The Management of Human Relations

BASIC MANAGEMENT SERIES

GENERAL EDITORS

Huxley Madeheim
City University of New York

Edward M. Mazze
Pennsylvania State University

Charles S. Stein
Continental Paper Company

The
Management
of
Human
Relations

SAUL W. GELLERMAN
IBM World Trade Corporation

HOLT, RINEHART AND WINSTON
NEW YORK   CHICAGO   SAN FRANCISCO   TORONTO   LONDON

FOR ELIZABETH GRACE

Editors' Foreword

The Basic Management Series is an authoritative collection of books intended for supplementary textbook use in basic management courses, in advanced management courses at the undergraduate or graduate level, and in combination as a basic textbook for principles of management courses. The advantages of such a series of concise books is that they give the instructor flexibility in building a course that will expose his students to varied points of view and approaches to management as well as to some current research findings. Short, supplementary books help to strengthen and bring up-to-date standard basic management textbooks.

The individual books in the series are self-contained treatments of important subject areas in management. The books include both theoretical and practical materials. The series introduces students to the writings of leading specialists in the field of management who have both academic and practical experience.

Two books serving as an introduction to the series are *Management Science* and *Management Controls*. Three books treat aspects of the management of human resources: *Organization Theory, The*

Management of Human Relations, and *Executive Control*. A key policy area of management is covered by *Industrial Relations*. *Integrated Manufacturing* provides an overview of the management of production. A frontier area in management is examined in *International Management*. All books in the series may use *Management Workbook* and *Cases in Management* for supplementary material.

The Basic Management Series is based on the idea that the study and practice of management are changing fundamentally as a result of the accelerated rate of change in the environment surrounding management action and the explosion of knowledge in business-related disciplines. It is hoped that the books in the series will stimulate the student to independent thought in the study of management as a discipline.

HUXLEY MADEHEIM
EDWARD M. MAZZE
CHARLES S. STEIN

Preface

The manager who would have an effective influence on the behavior of the people he supervises must first learn to analyze their situations realistically. A sound analysis leads to appropriate action and usually to an appropriate response by the people involved.

This formulation of human relations seems simple enough, but in real life it is exceedingly difficult. Many of our beliefs about how people should be managed are shrouded in misconceptions and myths. These range from the traditionalists' attitude that people can be controlled by "the carrot and the stick,"—that is, by a system of rewards and punishments—to the more recent notion that to supervise effectively it is necessary "to like people and know how to handle them." There is a certain amount of truth in each of these ideas. However, neither is really adequate as an explanation for human relations problems in general or as a guide to the manager who faces these problems daily and must find solutions quickly.

Human relations, as a subject to be studied and an art to be practiced, is still emerging from its traditional mythologies into a more scientific era. There is still a long way to go. Research is continuing to

reveal a very complex set of influences that affect the attitudes, interpersonal relationships, and productivity of people at work. But the important point is that a systematic understanding of all these variables, which is not yet within our grasp, would make possible a much more productive and, at the same time, a much more satisfying and humane industrial order.

This book is intended as an introduction to the current state of this important, and rapidly evolving, branch of management. It is intended to be practical and down-to-earth, while at the same time placing research and theory in their proper perspective. As both a practicing industrial psychologist and a manager in a large corporation, I live, as it were, in both the scientific and the practical worlds. I have tried to blend both of these viewpoints in this book.

Any introductory text must choose between omitting a number of potentially interesting subjects or trying to cover too many subjects in what might be a superficial way. I have chosen the former strategy. My aim was to cover in some depth the most serious and common, although not necessarily the most dramatic, problems facing managers in today's industry.

S. W. G.

New York, N.Y.
November 1965

Contents

The Management of Human Relations

Introduction

The Importance of Human Relations

Human relations is simply a catch-all term for describing the way in which the people who comprise an organization think about each other and deal with each other. These relations may be considered good when they enhance the likelihood that the organization will reach its goals and poor when they do not. There are many reasons why human relations is an important concern of management, and it will be the main purpose of this opening section to review some of them. But we should state at the outset that the chief importance of human relations to management is that *they are manageable*. Although this statement may seem so self-evident as to be trivial, if we examine it a bit more deeply, it will soon become clear that we are saying something here that is both controversial and profound. Indeed we are contradicting a good deal of management experience and of so-called common sense.

History, of course, is full of strikes, turnover, deliberately restricted production, and other forms of unproductive behavior. These seem, on the surface, to support the belief that human nature is hard-

ly a worthwhile topic for a practical man to study. But modern management theory has made a complete departure from this traditional viewpoint, and this has come about largely for two reasons: (1) Social research during the last three decades has made on-the-job behavior a great deal more intelligible than it used to be. (2) Partly as a result of this research, our conception of the process of management has changed.

Until recently there were very few explicit theories of how people at work should be managed. However, two main methods were employed, and these implied certain underlying assumptions about human nature. One of these was the method of coercion, which used the threat of dismissal as a means of compelling an economically dependent individual to behave more or less as his employers wanted. The other was the method of *compensation,* which used the reward of money (or of other benefits that cost money, such as insurance or prizes) as a means of attracting the individual toward activities which would help his employer. Although one method was negative in its approach and the other was positive, both assumed that most people had to be subjected to some form of external control in order to be productive in their jobs. The individual had to be disciplined or tempted or both. Management seemed to consist of learning how best to play on human fears and appetites in order to regulate behavior. We might therefore summarize the traditional management approach to human relations by saying that it regarded people as more or less incomprehensible, and that it dealt with them by what amounted to manipulation. Coercion and compensation are still with us, of course, and they probably always will be. They are, however, no longer regarded as especially potent motivators, except under certain circumstances; they are certainly not considered to be sufficient in themselves for obtaining employee cooperation or stimulating morale.

The modern concept of human relations is considerably subtler than the traditional one. It is based on the idea that no belief is illogical to the man who believes in it and that no deed is unjustified in the mind of the man who does it. Therefore, it is not the responsibility of the manager to judge the relative degree of rightness of an employee's action with an eye toward reward or punishment. Rather, he must try to understand *why* the employee acts or believes as he does so that the underlying causes can be dealt with. Instead of reacting to superficial symptoms with equally superficial cures, the modern manager tries to get at the roots of behavior and to introduce any desired changes at that level. The new approach to human relations does not

consist of a set of techniques for handling people but of an analytic approach to understanding them. Precisely because the behavior of people on the job *can* be understood, and because the manager does *not* have to be a psychologist or a human relations expert to understand it, we can assert with some assurance that *human relations are manageable.*

Effects of Human Relations

So far, however, we have only said that the management of human relations is possible; we have not shown why it is valuable. An effective program of human relations can in fact be immensely valuable to any organization. The quality of human relations can have an important effect on productivity and creativity and therefore on the profitability and efficiency of an enterprise. This does not imply that "happy" employees are necessarily more productive than "unhappy" ones. As we shall see later, the relationship between productivity and morale is quite complex. For one thing, a worker's actual output is affected by many factors that are not directly related to his attitudes. These may include his training, the condition of his tools, and the care that has gone into the planning of his part in the total production process. Further, it is easy to fall into semantic traps when discussing so intangible a factor as morale. For example, a worker who has high morale is not necessarily happy in the sense of contentment or open enthusiasm. Morale is best understood as one's attitude toward accomplishing his work, rather than as the emotions he displays during work.

Despite these difficulties, there is good reason to believe that an organization whose members experience a sense of dignity in their jobs will usually be more productive than an organization in which such feelings do not occur. Sometimes the advantage is quite clear, as in the case of higher volume or lower scrap costs. Sometimes it is less tangible, as in the case of increases in ingenuity, cooperation, or persistance. However it is manifested, the productivity advantages of good human relations are often directly translatable into dollars and cents. Since so many of any company's costs are directly affected by the intentions of its employees, it is sound business policy to keep those intentions positive. It may be difficult to pinpoint the effects of human relations in a profit and loss statement, but the realistic manager knows that they are there.

If good human relations can make a company more efficient,

does it follow that bad human relations can make it less efficient? Indeed it does. The sometimes catastrophic results of low morale are much easier to demonstrate than the subtler effects of high morale. Even when it cannot be clearly shown that favorable attitudes bring tangible advantages to a particular company, it is well worth trying to foster them as insurance against the penalties that low morale can bring.

The most dramatic of these penalties are strikes. These are usually reported in the press as being caused by either disputes over wages or fringe benefits or by issues that can effect earnings such as work rules or job security. Indeed, many strikes are entirely economic in origin and are due to the inability of a buyer and a seller (management and labor) to agree on a price. But many strikes cannot be explained so easily: they are not so much a matter of economic disagreement as of mutual suspicion, mistrust, or misunderstanding. A company whose employees have chronically unfavorable opinions of their management may find itself involved in strikes over relatively trivial issues. In this sense, some companies can be considered strikeprone, because each side is accustomed to regarding the other as an enemy whose every move is a potential attack. In companies with high fixed costs, or companies whose market position requires that they maintain reliable delivery schedules, the cost of such suspicion can be devastating.

Excessive turnover is another common result of low morale, especially in times when other job opportunities are abundant. Because of the cost of recruiting and training new employees, turnover can cause a serious drain on a company's assets. This drain is often more serious than a normal cost accounting can show. For example, the loss of a highly trained specialist (for whom other job opportunities are nearly always abundant) costs a great deal more than just the money required to find his replacement. It delays the projects he was working on; if he was a singularly gifted person, the project may have to be postponed indefinitely. Worse still, his departure may convince other specialists outside the company that it is not a desirable place to work. Therefore, the very act of leaving may deprive the company not only of an employee but of access to suitable replacements as well. High turnover is often treated as a problem in employee selection rather than in morale. In many cases, improved selection methods can reduce turnover, especially where it is due to inadequate skill or aptitude. But it is not always wise for companies to search for new tests or selection methods when they lose too many dissatisfied

people. This strategy very often amounts to looking for a test that can identify people who are willing to tolerate an intolerable situation. The wise manager looks at both the people *and* the work situation before deciding on the cause of the mismatch.

Restriction of output is another common result of poor morale. It is harder to measure than turnover, and sometimes it can be so cleverly concealed that management may not be aware of the extent to which it is happening. The deliberate limitation of production by employees is as old as the industrial revolution itself. Originally it was caused by fear of producing more than the market can absorb ("working yourself out of a job") or of incurring a reduction in wage rates. In modern industry, job security is frequently guaranteed by union contracts or at least implied by custom; wage rates are more often based on hours or months worked than on quantity of production. Nevertheless, deliberate restriction of production is still very much a part of the industrial scene for a variety of reasons. Sometimes it is done in order to avoid too wide a disparity between the wages of the highest and lowest paid employees. Working people are by no means the economic men that traditional management presumed them to be. When a system of incentive payments appears to give some workers an unfair advantage over the rest, the favored ones often hold production back to the extent necessary to keep wages more or less in line. However, attempts by employees to keep production within certain limits can also occur where wages are not paid on an incentive basis. Regardless of the setting in which it occurs, restriction of output by employees seems to serve the same general purpose: to exert a degree of control over the job environment and to offset, at least to some extent, management's seemingly overwhelming control of that environment. If the workers in a company regard their management as untrustworthy, they will resort to restriction of output as a way of protecting themselves. On the other hand, if they regard management as fair and reliable, they are much more likely to cooperate in various engineering or time-and-motion studies designed to increase their productivity.

The Environment of Industry

So far we have been discussing the effects which human relations can have on the operating efficiency of a firm. There is another set of reasons illustrating why human relations should be a continuing concern of management, and although these are not related to efficiency,

they may in the long run prove to be a more important consideration than any of the others. Broadly speaking, these are concerned with the need to build an industrial democracy that is consistent with the ideals of political democracy and that helps to sustain those ideals.

It is our cultural attitudes toward economic issues—employment, investment, profit, taxes, and productivity—that largely determine the economic environment in which organizations of all kinds must operate. When we consider that nearly all adults in a mature industrial economy are either employed or dependent on someone who is employed, it becomes clear that the attitudes of employees can affect far more than just the internal operations of a company. Attitudes are the stuff of which human relations are built. They can also become part of a general consensus throughout the economy that can approve or disapprove the way in which it is being run. In the long run, this consensus *is* the external environment in which the company must somehow find its place, prosper, and survive.

To the extent that on-the-job experiences can affect these attitudes, the quality of human relations in a company has a slow but inexorable effect on the willingness of society at large to tolerate that company and other companies like it. Therefore, it is clear that profits that are earned at the expense of dignity can be self-defeating; that the pride, self-fulfillment, and satisfaction of employees must be one of the main concerns of any enlightened business. This is not a matter of coddling or of soft management at all but a simple confrontation with the hard facts of life. A business that neglects the feelings of its employees alters its own environment until it is finally unable to adapt itself to the changes it has made.

This problem has been recognized for some time, and a number of methods have been evolved for dealing with it. Some companies have tried to educate both their own employees and the public at large about the advantages of the free enterprise system. Others have sought to make wage payments as high as possible and to supplement these wages with as generous a package of fringe benefits as they could afford. Other companies, while not neglecting education and compensation, have based their human relations program on the belief that employee satisfaction or dissatisfaction is centered on the worker's daily experience with his job, his superiors, and his fellow employees.

This book will be largely devoted to discussing the reasons why concern about employee satisfaction is the most realistic approach and to reviewing the specific ways in which the approach can be applied.

Obstacles to Good Human Relations

The advantages of good human relations are now widely recognized, and many companies have made deliberate attempts to improve their employees' morale and loyalty. However, the results of these efforts are often disappointing. Good human relations are not easy to achieve or maintain and for several reasons. First, many attempts to improve the working climate in an organization are based on some rather naive ideas. One such idea is that most people respond well to a personal approach, and therefore the key to better attitudes is to teach the supervisor some new verbal etiquette. For example, he may be taught to call employees by their first names, to memorize a few facts about their families so he can ask about their health, and above all to praise the employees' work at every opportunity. All this sweetness is unlikely to do any harm, but neither is it likely to produce any significant changes in morale. Very few supervisors are capable actors, and if their interest is transparently insincere it will earn them either contempt or laughter. Even when the supervisor is genuinely friendly, experience has shown that employee morale needs a great deal more stimulation than can be provided just by saying the right things to them.

Another naive idea, which is frequently thought of as a cure for poor employee relations, is that man is basically a pecuniary animal, and therefore his morale can be bought. Some firms make it a practice to pay high wages and to pointedly remind employees of this if they complain about other aspects of their work. Other companies have granted general pay increases in response to indications that their men were disgruntled. This is usually done on the assumption that the men are probably unhappy about money; even if their real problem lies elsewhere, they will presumably forget about it in their joy over receiving more pay.

Although money can be a powerful motivator, it sometimes motivates people in unforeseen ways. When it is used to intimidate a man, as in the first case, it will very often induce him to seek revenge. He can do this openly by resigning from the company or more subtly by permitting an important piece of work to be done poorly, especially when the defect is hard to notice or to trace. When money is used to silence a complaint, as in the second example, it can lead to the impression that the management did not understand what the employees' problems really were. It can also imply that complaints can be an easy way of generating pay increases.

There is certainly nothing wrong with courtesy or with money as means of dealing with employees. The difficulty lies in the fact that they are so often prescribed as panaceas, and are quite insufficient to bring about any lasting attitude changes among employees. The average working man is not a child who can be cajoled or bribed into forgetting about something that troubles him. He is an adult with a certain amount of pride, complex emotional needs, and a long memory for insults. His superiors would be on dangerous ground if they expected to pacify him by performing a few diverting tricks with words or money.

A second reason why good relations with employees are often difficult to achieve is that the supervisor, being human, may have some qualities that make him rather hard to like. Unfortunately, the possession of authority brings out the worst in some men. Sometimes, especially when a supervisor is relatively inexperienced, he may feel it necessary to reinforce his authority by reserving all decisions for himself or by adhering to his decisions even after they have clearly been shown to be unwise. Although he may think that his firmness has given his men a good demonstration of just who is boss, it is much more likely to give the impression that he is a martinet (a judgment which is usually expressed in more colorful terms).

It is easy to criticize the personalities of supervisors or their training, and indeed it is a common habit of higher management to do exactly that. But it is well to remember that first-line supervision is one of the most demanding jobs in all of industry. The supervisor is charged with getting a job done through men who are unlikely to respect him until and unless he can prove that he deserves it. Between the need of his men to defend *their* egos against his domination, and the supervisor's own need to defend *his* ego against their unwillingness to accept his leadership, there can be very little room left for compromise. To establish an effective working relationship in these circumstances calls for uncommon patience, wisdom, and fairness. It is scarcely any wonder that the relationships between employees and their supervisors are often little more than an uneasy truce, and that the atmosphere of mutual trust that writers on human relations are so fond of advocating is all too rare. Indeed, supervisors who have learned to create mutually supportive relationships with their men deserve a great deal of credit.

There is, in other words, a psychologically difficult situation inherent in all relationships where one adult exercises authority over another adult. This is especially true in the United States, where a

strong egalitarian tradition teaches one to cherish his independence and to assume that no one is really entitled to tell one what to do. The typical American reaction to the realities of industrial life includes a certain amount of irritation, a certain unwillingness to cooperate with supervisors to a greater extent than necessary, and above all, a reluctance to confide in them.

The tendency of employees to keep information to themselves and even to deliberately deceive their supervisors is quite common. Although it is sometimes provoked by agitators and more often by needlessly arrogant supervisors, this reluctance to communicate is usually nothing more sinister than an attempt by the employees to preserve their dignity against what *seems* like unwarranted interference in their own affairs. Regardless of its cause, the failure of employees to communicate fully with their supervisors is a serious handicap for management, and it immensely complicates the job of improving human relations. One of the most insidious ways in which secretiveness on the part of employees affects human relations is by creating the illusion that since no one is complaining, all must be well. Even experienced managers have fallen into this trap. When employees have very little to say to their supervisors, it is *not* necessarily an indication that they are satisfied. It is all too easy for managers to take the position that they should "let sleeping dogs lie" when their men seem to be quiescent. Many managers have resisted proposals that they should investigate the reasons for the silence on the grounds that to do so might stir up the employees and cause them to think too much about conditions that they might otherwise be content to accept.

The lack of spontaneous feedback about job attitudes from employees to their managers, far from indicating that the men are contented, can also be a symptom of sullen unwillingness to trust management or of despair that management would give them a fair hearing. This unwillingness of employees to reveal their feelings deprives management of an invaluable "early warning system" by means of which potentially serious misunderstandings can be detected and avoided.

That this "silence" is still so widely misunderstood is in itself a symptom of three serious obstacles to establishing good human relations. First, it is unfortunately true that *some managers have not learned to recognize good morale when they see it.* Good morale is not marked by the absence of complaints but rather by the nature of the complaints that are made and by the manner in which they are expressed. In general, when morale is high there is likely to be a moder-

ate amount of complaining about things which make it difficult to get the job done properly, such as parts shortages or inadequate tools; this tends to be expressed in a bantering manner that has at least a touch of good humor in it. On the other hand, when morale is deteriorating there are likely to be complaints about the inadequacy of the rewards which the employees receive for their work, such as unfair wages or insufficient free time. These complaints are likely to be expressed with an air of rancor and contentiousness. And when morale is seriously depressed, the employees are likely to complain among themselves of nearly everything connected with their work; they will not reveal this directly to management because they either fear reprisals or doubt that anything can be gained through frankness. Men in this state of mind feel the need of a spokesman and for this reason tend to be receptive to efforts by labor unions to organize them.

The second obstacle to good human relations concerns the lack of understanding of the psychological importance of complaining itself. It is an old axiom in the military services that a certain amount of griping is normal and even desirable, and the experienced sergeant is more concerned about too little griping than about too much. This is because there are frustrations that are inherent in belonging to any organization, if only because no organization can permit its members to behave entirely as they please. To complain of frustrations, even petty ones, is often a harmless way of working off the tensions that these frustrations bring. Especially when the complaints are tinged with humor, they can help to make the burdens of organized life more bearable.

But if a complaint can relieve tensions for the employee, it can create tensions for the supervisor. It is all too easy for him to interpret a complaint as an indictment of the way he has done his job and to assume that he must defend himself against the dissatisfied employee rather than regard the dissatisfaction as a symptom of something deeper. Therefore, the supervisor may seek to either dismiss the employee's complaints or to discredit them; since many complaints lack a strong factual basis, this is not a difficult task. But by effectively defending his own actions, the supervisor may only succeed in frustrating the employees still further because they were seeking a hearing rather than a change.

Third, there is a tendency, which we have already hinted at, of being "captured" by one's role. A role is the expected behavior associated with a position in a particular system. For example, a teacher's role is usually considered to be helpful and guiding, while a police-

man's role is watchful and enforcing. There are many roles in our business, family, and extracurricular lives, and in playing them we all tend to adopt a style which blends our own personalities with the demands we feel the role makes upon us. It is no longer very clear as to just what constitutes the expected behavior of a supervisor. While the stereotype of the old-fashioned straw boss who demands complete obedience is still with us, it has clearly gone out of fashion. On the other hand, the so-called "human-relations–oriented" supervisor can turn out to be a lax disciplinarian with a ready smile and a poor production record. There is, in other words, a certain ambiguity as to what is expected of a supervisor. In practice, this means that some supervisors vacillate between "tough" and "tender" approaches to their men, while others dispense with role-playing altogether and supervise according to their natural inclinations, be they tough, tender, or whatever.

Oddly enough, the knack of supervising in one's natural style is not easy to learn. Further, unless that style is either downright nasty or outrageously indulgent, it may be at least as conducive to good morale as a more contrived and "proper" approach. When a man knows that his performance in a position is being watched and judged, the temptation to play a role rather than to trust his instincts can be enormous. Unfortunately, this only serves to make him unpredictable as far as his men are concerned. Since an artificial style is hard to maintain consistently, he is likely to use it only some of the time. Therefore, what he thinks of as supervisory artistry may only persuade his men of his insincerity and make them skeptical of his intentions toward them.

Too often, however, a supervisor will become so captured by the role he thinks he should be playing that he loses sight of the real reasons for his having been given that role in the first place. For example, he may think of his relations with his men as a contest between adversaries or as a performance by one active and thinking man before a passive and apathetic audience. He may feel that he must accomplish the group's tasks by himself, using the group as a sort of unwilling tool. These notions have an unfortunate way of becoming self-fulfilling prophecies: If you treat a man as an adversary, he will become one. If you credit a man with little or no spirit or intelligence, he will not bother to reveal any. In this way the unwary supervisor can become caught in a circle of his own making. If he affects his men in ways that cause them to confirm his erroneous ideas about them, he makes his own job harder and harder and drives his

men farther and farther away from him. Instead of building team spirit and pride of accomplishment, he builds enmity and a perverse delight in thwarting him.

These, then, are several reasons why good human relations are difficult to attain. To some extent it is a matter of unenlightened practices; to a greater extent it is due to the difficulties inherent in imposing an organized system of conduct onto any group of individuals and to the peculiar ways in which individuals manage to preserve their dignity when they find themselves part of such a system. It follows from this that the problems of human relations in industry are too complex and subtle to be dealt with in a simple way. A manager only deceives himself if he believes that these problems will vanish if he applies a few doses of supervisory training or of better communications or of wage increases or any other favorite nostrum. But this does not mean that human relations problems are insoluble. It only means that solving them calls for a more careful and informed analysis than they have received in the past. It is the main purpose of this book to help the student learn to make such analyses and above all to convince him that they are necessary.

The next four chapters of this book are basically theoretical, and the last five chapters are basically practical or "applied." The intent of this format is to give the student a good grounding in human relations theory without pursuing it in great detail, and to concentrate on the major human relations problems that managers face on an everyday basis.

CHAPTER TWO

Background of the Human Relations Movement

The human relations movement today takes its shape from several historical elements. Five broad factors have helped to set the stage: (1) the movement of labor from agriculture to industry; (2) the reform movements that developed in reaction to early entrepreneurial excesses; (3) the rise of labor unions and labor legislation; (4) the tendency of competitive, profit-seeking industry to encourage technology, which in turn stimulates and is further stimulated by education; and (5) the professionalization of management, bringing with it specialized management education and social research.

The Flow of Labor

What we call industrialization became possible when farmers began to move off the farm land and into the towns, thus creating a labor supply. This movement started for various reasons: sometimes

there were too many people for the land to support or there were developed more profitable uses for the land, such as sheep-raising. The earliest movement away from the farm was not a matter of choice but of compulsion. Therefore, the men who became the millhands in the early factories were a dispossessed and bewildered lot, usually lacking both the skills that could have made them productive and the bargaining power that could have protected their economic interests. Accordingly they worked long hours for low wages and usually eked out a very miserable existence indeed.

This earliest stage of industrialization had two important consequences, which are with us to this day. One was the rise of Marxist ideology, which considered the exploitation of labor to be a necessary result of the private ownership of capital. If the changes wrought by industrialization had stopped at that early stage, Marx's predictions of increasing class conflict and eventual revolution would undoubtedly have been far more accurate than history has actually shown them to be. The second consequence was a confirmation of the old feudal class relationships in a different form: where the serfs had formerly been subordinate to and dependent on the nobility, the working class became, if anything, even more dependent on the enterpreneurial class. Wtih class consciousness came a profound difference in attitudes between the payers and the receivers of wages. Since in Europe this difference was superimposed directly on the old feudal relationships, it has persisted there much more strongly than in the United States where this relationship never actually existed. However, even in America there are important differences in the ways that workers and proprietors think about each other. Broadly speaking, the proprietor tends to think of employees in terms of his responsibility to meet the payroll, that is, as a burden. The employee tends to think of the proprietor in terms of his own security, that is, as a benefactor who is always a potential malefactor. A great deal of conflict still results from this difference.

The flow of manpower off the land into the industrial towns still continues, but in advanced economies another flow tends to become far more significant. This is the movement of workers out of manufacturing jobs into administrative and service jobs. The structure of the economy changes, in other words, from labor-intensive to capital-intensive production. This brings with it a corresponding change in the job structure: there are more jobs requiring a high order of skill and paying high wages and relatively fewer low-skilled and low-wage jobs.

As a result, an increasing proportion of the labor force finds itself secure and affluent, and this brings with it important changes in attitudes. Professional satisfactions and prestige become relatively more important, while the size of the paycheck becomes relatively less important. As an economy becomes more productive, the relationship of the average man to his work becomes less of a grim struggle for existence and more of a search for self-actualization.

The historical evolution of the labor force from dispossessed farmers to unskilled millhands to more or less "professionalized" specialists has had a profound impact on what we have come to call human relations. First, there is the proletarian heritage of dependency and immobility, which expresses itself today in an emphasis on security and a tendency for workers to band together informally to control production. Second, there is the entrepreneurial heritage of self-sufficiency and profit seeking, which tends to regard the dependent worker as lazy and shortsighted. From this opinion flows the traditional managerial view that the average working man must be stimulated and disciplined and even protected against his own foolishness. Third, there is the more recent tendency for well-paid workers to be frustrated by work that is dull, and to be unimpressed by efforts to satisfy them by adding further material benefits. This is due in part to a tendency for human relations practices to lag behind changes in the motivation of the work force by several years, so that today's workers tend to receive yesterday's rewards.

The ideas that are prevalent about human relations today are therefore the results of experience gained at several different levels of economic development. Since the economy is not uniform but contains vestiges of nearly all previous forms of employment, the needs and attitudes of workers are quite heterogenous. Therefore we cannot generalize about what all working people want or how all working people think. We can generalize, however, about the directions in which history has been flowing: It shows a movement away from absolute dependency on the employer toward a search for significance in one's work. It moves away from conflict between workers and employers toward increasingly uniform goals held by professionalized workers and equally professional managers. The slow, broad sweep of history is making the human relations problems of the late nineteenth century increasingly irrelevant, just as it introduces new and difficult problems in the mid-twentieth century.

Reform Movements

Changes in the human relations movement did not come about entirely because of structural changes in the economy. To a considerable degree they occurred because of deliberate efforts to improve the condition of the working man. History moves far too slowly to satisfy the zealous reformer, and it can be shown that present-day human relations practices are as much the result of conscience as they are of economics. The callous attitude of early industrialists toward the worker did not go unchallenged for long. Reactions took many forms, some of them more effective than others, but they all combined in the long run to produce a climate of public opinion which directed attention to the rights of workers.

Even in the early days there were efforts to alleviate the lot of the working people. Many more or less utopian experiments were attempted, which varied in method but had the common aim of trying to organize society in a way that would overcome the inequities and abuses of the industrial world. Although none of these had a lasting effect on the industrial world as a whole, and very few even survived for very long, they led to a lasting search for more practical ways to organize a better society. Some of these utopias failed because they considered industrial methods themselves to be the main villain and tried to eliminate them by reverting to more primitive methods of production. In effect, they cured the disease by killing the patient. Some failed because they expected too sweeping a change in human nature to follow from the relief of economic hardships. Still others failed because they were based on theories that were far too grand or abstruse for ordinary men to live by. But in the long run, the most important thing about the utopian experiments is not that they failed but that they were attempted at all. The impulse to improve the lot of man is a lasting and pervasive influence in human history: for every cold-blooded cynic who held that most men were scoundrels deserving of no better than they got, there has been at least one high-minded visionary who believed that if men were fallible, they were also perfectible. While most of the attempts to build utopian societies were impractical or overly ambitious, they represented powerful religious and moral forces which could not be deterred by the failure of a few experiments. Eventually these forces chose a more practical route to their goal than a wholesale revision of society. They concentrated instead on the gradual reform of attitudes and practices.

Thus today's society, while it is hardly utopian by anybody's standards, is considerably more agreeable to more people than the era in which industrialization began. The economic forms of today's society have evolved from the older forms, but are not radically different; what has changed is not so much the forms of ownership as the prevailing attitudes toward the obligations of employers to their employees. Modern society understands its own dynamics better than the older society did, and a broader distribution of income and a far greater number of personal success stories has been the result.

The more practical routes which the reforming impulse followed included journalistic and literary appeals, political and religious action, and legislation. A whole literature of exposé and criticism grew up around the *muckrakers* in the early part of the twentieth century. While the critiques were not confined to labor practices, they set the tone for many subsequent writings that aroused public sympathy for the industrial employee. As public opinion became increasingly favorable toward action in behalf of the worker, the threat of restrictive legislation became increasingly likely. A few far-sighted managements moved to provide decent wages and working conditions in advance of that legislation. The National Labor Relations Act of 1935 created a powerful free labor movement that was quite able to look after its own interests and those of its members. In fact, organized labor became so powerful that public opinion began to react to some of its excesses, and this resulted in the Taft-Hartley Act of 1947 and the Landrum-Griffin Act of 1959. Both of these acts had the effect of counteracting some of the powers that had originally been granted to labor unions. However, the fundamental rights of labor are solidly established, and the organized worker need no longer depend solely on public sympathy or partisan journalists to defend his interests. Even the unorganized worker is indirectly protected by a powerful free labor movement, since the very possibility that its employees may be organized if they become too dissatisfied is a potent stimulus for a company to see to it that such dissatisfaction does not occur.

Labor Unions

The rise of labor unions and the passage of labor legislation has been the most dramatic and controversial effort made to improve the lot of industrial workers. Although there were sporadic efforts to organize workers during the early part of the century, union organization on a large scale did not begin until after the passage of the National

Labor Relations Act. Prior to that time unions had waged an essentially defensive struggle, partly to assert their right to exist and partly to protect their members against the power of management. However, it was not only the absence of legislative sponsorship that inhibited the early growth of the unions. Company managements were, on the whole, steadfastly opposed to them, and many tactics that are legally defined today as unfair labor practices were employed to discourage employees from joining unions. These ranged from intimidation of striking workers to armed attacks by company guards. While the strikers nearly always lost these battles, in the end they won the war. Public revulsion against these tactics eventually paved the way for the acceptance of unions as a permanent fixture on the industrial scene.

The industrial workers were not, at first, overly interested in unions. Since there was very little precedent for them, it was not clear whether unions would bring any important advantages. Further, in a country which was still largely agricultural and where many industrial workers had been raised in essentially rural settings, labor unions had unattractive overtones of being foreign and even conspiratorial. The efforts of socialists and communists to promote the growth of unions not only made many working people suspicious of unions, but also left a taint of unrespectability even long after the extreme left wing had ceased to play an important role in union affairs.

Gradually, as the country became more industrial and urban, resistance to unions on the part of the workers themselves began to decrease. By 1904, there were about two million union members in the United States; this figure grew slowly to about five million in 1920. During the next decade, effective antiunion drives by large employers, often with government aid, had the effect of reducing union membership to less than three million by 1933. By then, however, the shock of the great depression with its severe unemployment (about twenty-five percent of the labor force was out of work in 1933, and five years later the jobless rate was still about twenty percent) had helped to make American workers considerably more militant. The ferocity of the antiunion drives backfired in the end by arousing a stubbornly prounion spirit among many working people who felt that their rights had been outraged and abused. That there was no longer any great reluctance by industrial workers to organize was clearly demonstrated by the rapid growth of union membership after the National Labor Relations Act affirmed the right of collective bargaining and banned coercive acts against union members. Union membership

rose to a peak of around eighteen million (about one third of all non-farm workers) by the late 1950s. During this period, unions shifted from the defensive to the offensive. They underwent an aggressive growth in not only membership but also in financial resources and economic and political power.

Despite their unquestioned organizing success and their important economic impact, labor unions have encountered three serious difficulties: 1) the relative indifference and apathy of many union members; (2) the inability of unions to expand into nonmanufacturing employee groups and the effect of this failure on union membership; and (3) the public and legislative reaction to various union excesses.

Perhaps because unions have been so successful in winning their major economic battles, there is a tendency for many members to take their unions for granted and to ignore all but the most crucial union meetings. Many union locals have difficulty in bringing out a quorum for regular meetings. In effect, there is a tendency for many workers to regard their union not as a mutual protective alliance with other workers, but rather as a bargaining service that they buy. Union membership has lost much of its earlier fervor and has become, in many cases, something very much like casualty insurance.

Nearly all of the successful union organizing drives in the United States have taken place among so-called blue-collar workers in manufacturing industries. In 1964 they accounted for about 87 percent of all union memberships. However, employment in these types of jobs has been declining, largely due to automation. Meantime, the so-called white-collar jobs have been increasing, but labor unions have never been very successful in organizing these workers. The net effect of these changes has been a decline in union membership as a percentage of the total labor force. (From 1956 to 1963 there was also a decline in the absolute number of union members.) There are many reasons for the relative failure of labor unions to gain an important position among white-collar workers. A recent study by Albert A. Blum of Michigan State University cites these: (a) poorly chosen tactics by labor in appealing to office workers, which created more resentment than interest; (b) inability of many union organizers who have factory backgrounds themselves to understand the motives of white-collar workers: (c) effective management policies in maintaining a high degree of satisfaction among office workers; and (d) a tendency for white-collar workers to identify with management.(1)

During the years immediately following World War II, labor unions began to fall out of favor with the general public and with leg-

islators alike. There were many reasons for this, but perhaps the three main ones were: (1) the feeling that unions had fostered price inflation by demanding wage increases that were in excess of productivity increases, (2) disclosures that certain unions were dominated by racketeers and others by communists, and (3) a strong reaction (especially in the less industrialized states) against closed shop contracts, which require that all employees in an affected company become union members.

Inflationary problems have been at least partially resolved by governmental pressures to keep wage increases within noninflationary limits. The unions themselves had made strenuous if not entirely successful efforts to clean their own houses of undesirable elements. The closed shop was restricted by the Taft-Hartley Act, which authorized the states to ban such practices within their own borders.

The following observation was made in 1959 (the year of the Landrum-Griffin Act) by a mission from the International Labor Organization that visited the United States:

It is not uncommon for the mass of union members to be completely apathetic or tolerant toward their leaders' behavior. Some of them—among the more honest but less belligerent—are scared of losing their jobs; others are blinded by the real gains their union has won for them; while others feel that these gains compensate for their leaders' misdeeds. Moreover, expulsion, which is often the only way open to unions and their leaders wishing to get rid of undesirable elements, is a weapon that cuts both ways and its effectiveness is somewhat doubtful. (2:139)

The effect of these three factors (apathy, membership decline, and degree of public acceptance) has been to gradually blunt the aggressiveness of the unions' approach to management. If unions are not actually on the defensive, then they are in an increasingly conservative position. To the extent that their members have become "customers" rather than ardent supporters, they must increasingly render services to existing members rather than push the so far fairly fruitless search for new members. These services include not only the orthodox functions of bargaining and handling grievances but also the administration of various welfare functions. In effect, the role of the unions seems to be evolving from that of a militant champion of disadvantaged workers toward that of a discreet servant of relatively affluent and complacent clients. This does not imply that unions are going to become unimportant, much less fade from the industrial scene. But it does show that there is nothing really fixed or permanent about human attitudes. In the relatively short span of sixty years, the atti-

tudes of workers toward unions have changed from suspicion to slow acceptance to militant support to relative apathy and a demand for service.

Technology and Education

Returning to the effects of economic changes on human relations, the last few decades have seen the emergence of unprecedented and extremely important trends. Of these, perhaps the most important is the interaction between mass education, technology, and economic growth. The term *interaction* as used here refers to a process in which several factors influence, and in turn are influenced by, each other.

Mass education was introduced early in the United States, probably not so much because its eventual economic effects were foreseen as because of religious and political reasons. Whatever its originating circumstances, mass primary education soon began to have important effects of its own. Specifically, it led to vast proliferation of secondary education, and later to widespread university education. This upward thrust of education occurred partly because of the increased demand for teachers and partly because a largely literate population demanded further educational opportunities. But the greatest force that pushed, and still pushes, educational expansion is social mobility. This is a sociological term referring to the movement of an individual from the social class into which he was born to a higher class—higher, that is, in terms of prestige, income, and opportunities. The United States inherited very few of the class distinctions of Europe. It is largely a nation of immigrants and descendants of immigrants, and these people quickly realized that education could be a vehicle *par excellence* for social mobility. Consequently the United States has always been favorably inclined to invest heavily in education. The expansion of university-level training began in earnest with the passage of the Morrill Act of 1862, which encouraged the states to open so-called "land grant" colleges. This act supported a steady trend toward increasing college enrollments. By 1962 some 4.6 million students were enrolled at 2040 universities, colleges, and junior colleges. As more and more college-trained workers enter the labor force, two important effects emerge: one economic and one motivational.

The economic effect is the possibility of much more sophisticated and productive industrial activities. Educated people can both operate and create complex new processes. They make new technology possible, and this leads to new ideas, wider markets, and above all

greater profits. This realization has touched off a race for high-talent manpower on the part of employers. In turn, the obvious advantages of a college education to the prospective employee has resulted in higher than ever demands on the educational system itself. Education, technology, and business, therefore, keep boosting one another with constant acceleration, the end of which (if any) is not in sight.

The motivational effect results from the wholesale transformation of the labor force into an increasingly sophisticated, inquiring, information-hungry group. Not only is a larger segment of the labor force trained to think for itself, but it is also better paid; in view of the continuing demand for talent, it is more economically independent than in the past. These changes have brought about what amounts to a motivational revolution, the full consequences of which are only beginning to be realized. Consider the term "labor force" itself. It is an economist's term referring to the aggregate of all gainfully employed (or employable) persons, from a chairman of the board to a ditchdigger. Today's labor force has a high and growing proportion of professional, managerial, and white collar workers. (Depending on how you define them, they constituted as much as forty-four percent of the labor force in 1962.) Although it was a perfectly adequate word when the term was coined, labor, with its connotations of unskilled physical efforts, is becoming increasingly inadequate as a description of what this labor force does. Its growing archaic quality is a measure of the extent to which the working population has changed.

With increased education and economic independence come new needs, which cannot be easily satisfied since they tend to be rather esoteric. First, there is a heightened need for an understanding of how one's job fits into the broader context of the organization and even society at large. It is not enough to tell an educated worker what to do; he must also be told *why*. Second, there is a need for variety and growth. A job that loses its challenge through familiarity, and does not lead to newer challenges, will either grind the educated man's zeal down to zero or, more likely, be abandoned for a better job. A common symptom of this feeling is the following statement, which (with its variants) is perhaps the most frequently heard complaint among well-educated employees in industry today: "I don't want to be a (current job title) for the rest of my life!" Even if that statement is easily understandable to today's student, it is nevertheless quite revolutionary in the light of economic history of all but the very recent past.

A third need that has emerged as a consequence of greater education is for new forms of recognition. Generally speaking, a man's accomplishments and importance can be acknowledged in three ways: by money, by status symbols, and by the nature of his job assignment. We have already noted how money tends to become a less potent motivator (though never an unimportant one) when total income rises beyond the point of immediate need so that a surplus begins to be accumulated. Actually, the barrier that money encounters is partly economic and partly psychological. The attractiveness of an increase in income seems to depend less on the absolute amount in question than on the ratio between the existing income and the prospective increase. Thus a fifty-dollar monthly increase may be quite attractive to a man earning 500 dollars a month, but trivial and even insulting to a man earning 1500 dollars a month. It costs more to give a meaningful raise to a man who is making a better-than-average salary than to a lower paid man. For this reason, and also because the income tax rate begins to accelerate rapidly at higher levels, salary increases become progressively less practical as a means of recognizing the work of an already well-paid man. Stock options or discounted stock purchase plans, because they offer potentially sizable capital gains, may offer effective means of monetary recognition. However, stock options are necessarily limited to a few key men and discount plans to a small percentage of each employee's income, so as not to harm the interests of outside stockholders. Commissions have considerable appeal for some people, but unless they are paid in addition to a sizable salary base, few men would want to risk the wide income fluctuations they bring for more than a few years. Cash awards or bonuses,when awarded selectively and in meaningful amounts, can serve as an effective way of emphasizing the organization's appreciation of what some men have done. Therefore,because the well-educated man is also likely to become a well-paid man, it is increasingly difficult to provide the recognition he needs through monetary means. Other means must be found to supplement the effect of money and to provide a convincing reassurance that a man's unique worth to his company is appreciated and remembered.

The increasing use of status symbols has become one way of supplying recognition, for highly paid employees. These may be any object or custom that conveys, whether intentionally or otherwise, some indication of a man's relative rank in the hierarchy of importance within his company: a job title, office furniture, a secretary, re-

served parking space, the key to the executive washroom. Status symbols are frequently laughed at and sometimes bitterly criticized. Both the laughter and the criticism are sometimes justified: people can go to absurd lengths in order to establish fine and frequently fictitious distinctions between themselves and others. Further, the very idea that status differences exist that require advertisement through external symbols has overtones of snobbism and discrimination. However, status symbols result from an important human need for frequent reminders (to one's self and to the rest of the world) of just how much dignity and deference one has *earned*. It is only when status symbols are presumptuous or ostentatious that they are objectionable. Otherwise, like the hero's medal and the graduate's diploma, they serve as a permanent form of applause which helps men to preserve themselves as individuals during the inevitable and lengthy periods when they seem to be taken for granted.

However, a more effective form of recognition in the long run than either money or status symbols is simply the jobs a man is given to do. Ironically, job assignments are also the most frequently overlooked form of recognition. Yet nothing bespeaks faith in a man's abilities louder than sending him on a truly challenging assignment, and nothing mocks a man more derisively than a highly paid and highly touted job that is essentially meaningless. This does not mean that it is necessary to keep moving a man to new jobs whenever the old one lapses into routine; although in the case of well-educated and highly motivated employees, that may be very desirable. It does mean that most jobs can be enlarged, especially in terms of planning and decision making; this enlargement can pay off in heightened motivation to at least as great a degree as the more conventional attempts to provide recognition.

In effect, then, the entry into the labor force of large numbers of highly educated men and women has made it necessary to completely rethink many of the time-honored notions about how to satisfy employees. In many companies it is still assumed, or at least not seriously questioned, that the policies that proved adequate in the days when most employees wore blue collars are still adequate today. Yet job security, a decent income, and decent working conditions only begin to express the needs of the well-educated workers. (It is not even clear any longer that they are all the blue collar worker needs, either.) Because of this time lag in management's recognition of motivational changes, there is a substantial supply of talented workers who are constantly on the lookout for new jobs.

Management Education and Social Research

Another important effect of economic change upon human relations practices is the professionalization of management. This began when companies grew too large and too complex to be managed effectively by the proprietor's family. The trend continued with the specialization of labor within management, which gradually created a welter of highly developed professions within what had once been a straightforward job of running a business. As management became a profession rather than a function of ownership, two important effects began to appear. The first was an increasing stress on results rather than on the prerogatives of being a manager. In order to achieve more profitable results, managers were willing to experiment and innovate. They were open to new ideas and indeed they actually sought them, especially among university faculties. Gradually, as management was enriched by inputs from the classical disciplines (economics, sociology, mathematics), it became both a subject for study by student managers and a subject for research by academicians. Despite a certain philistinism among some businessmen, and a certain air of cloistered aloofness among some faculty people, the links between business and the universities have become increasingly stronger. For both parties, the main reason for cooperative liaison is that it pays off in improved operating methods and in sponsorship of university projects, as well as mutual intellectual stimulation. This relationship has led directly to a large number of research projects in industrial human relations that have greatly illuminated the problems of attaining effective cooperation on the job.

The second effect of the professionalization of management was subtler. It became necessary to look for managerial personnel at all levels of society. Even though there had been a tendency (as in Europe) to keep class distinctions intact, the sheer pressures of economics have swept it aside. There was (and is) a greater need for managers than could be supplied by any one class, regardless of how capable its members might be. Although managers are not drawn equally from all sorts of social origins, they are a very diverse group with a wide variety of backgrounds. Managers began to appear who could understand the workers' attitudes because they themselves had lived in the conditions that molded those attitudes. It was easier for the professional manager to be compassionate and at the same time to recognize the practicality of winning the loyalty and respect of the

workers, than it had been for the hereditary managers of earlier generations. Therefore, at the same time that management was forging its links with the academic community, managers themselves were becoming considerably more receptive to an attempt to understand employees and to use this understanding as a tool for more effective management.

Thus the groundwork was laid for both social research in industry and for the widespread acceptance by managers of the human relations concepts that grew out of that research. By now there has been such a volume of this research that industrial sociology (or industrial social psychology) has become an academic discipline in its own right. It is the basis of much of the modern approach to human relations, and accordingly we will place considerable stress on research in this book. It is beyond the scope of this book to cover industrial social research in a comprehensive way; we will use certain selected studies to illustrate the concepts being presented.

Supervisory Styles

Of the several avenues that social research has followed in industry, the best known has been the study of supervisory styles and their effects on employees. Although this research has by now been pursued in many places, it is chiefly identified with the Harvard Graduate School of Business Administration and with the Institute for Social Research at the University of Michigan.

The most famous of all these studies was carried out at the Hawthorne works of the Western Electric Company in Chicago by the late Elton Mayo and his associates from Harvard between 1927 and 1932. The study is worth reviewing here for its historical significance. It caught the imagination of industrial leaders and succeeded, for the first time, in popularizing both social research itself and the modern concept of effective human relations. A great deal of subsequent research has used the Hawthorne studies as a point of departure or as a source of ideas and interpretations. The Hawthorne studies provide an excellent illustration of several important phenomena: restriction of output; informal work groups; the effects of the supervisor; and the so-called "Hawthorne effect" itself.

What Happened at Hawthorne

The occasion for these studies was a rather peculiar finding by a group of efficiency engineers who were experimenting with various methods of illuminating the work areas of several production departments. When they increased the illumination, the productivity of the workers rose; this probably pleased the engineers because that is what they expected. But what confounded them was the fact that productivity also rose when illumination was decreased or when it wasn't changed at all. Mayo was asked to look into this paradox, and his attempts to solve it opened the modern era of human relations.

Mayo's studies at Hawthorne had two main phases. One was an attempt to get around the baffling problem of inexplicable productivity increases seemingly generated by introducing rest periods. This was a false lead as it turned out, but Mayo was able to turn it into a classical instance of serendipity. Using orthodox experimental procedure, Mayo tried to hold constant all factors which might affect productivity (other than the factor he was investigating—fatigue). One of the extraneous factors that had to be controlled was the cooperativeness of the employees in the various groups under observation. To keep cooperativeness constant, Mayo let the workers in each experimental group decide for themselves the sequence in which each individual would take his rest period. Once again output soared in all groups, regardless of the amount of rest involved. Mayo was clever enough to realize that he had inadvertently released a very strong motivator through the simple act of letting the workers participate in the selection of their rest periods. He concluded that it was this participation, rather than the rest itself, which had made the difference.

But why had production gone up when the engineers had varied the lighting, particularly when there was no participation by the employees in deciding how it was to be varied? Mayo's answer was that in both the experiments—the effects of illumination and the merit of rest periods—the singling out of certain groups of employees for special attention had the effect of coalescing previously indifferent individuals into cohesive groups with a high degree of group pride or *esprit de corps*. Because of this pride, the workers were able to devote themselves wholeheartedly to their work. This was the famous Hawthorne effect that has by now been observed in an enormous variety of work settings: the very fact of receiving unaccustomed attention makes a group more conscious of itself and enhances its morale. This

effect is independent of the particular way in which the attention is manifested. In the case of the groups which chose their own rest periods, the Hawthorne effect received an extra boost from their participation in a decision affecting their work. This not only required them to act as a group, but more importantly, it also gave them a small but unprecedented degree of control over their jobs. To a limited extent, they became their own bosses. This struck a strongly responsive chord.

But why? To get the answer, Mayo and his associates launched the second phase of their research, which was an extremely comprehensive interview program among the Hawthorne employees. By the time this research had to be terminated because of the depression, it included about 20,000 separate interviews. As these progressed, it became apparent that life in the factory was a rather dismal affair and that life outside the factory was, for the worker, seldom much better. Again and again the interviews detected a feeling of futility and passive resignation among the workers. Something important was missing from their lives. A clue as to what the missing element was came from observations of how workers formed informal associations with each other during working hours. Mayo pursued this clue relentlessly, and while this resulted in extremely important insights it also led to some oversimplifications that persist to this day as to what human relations is all about.

The spontaneously formed informal work groups were, in Mayo's judgment, the key to the puzzle. He viewed them as a natural but inadequate defense against the stultifying anonymity of factory life: as an attempt to recapture some of the sense of belonging and of being welcome that had presumably pervaded the preindustrial farm families and craft shops. In brief, the modern industrial worker was confronted with a world that was indifferent to him and that dealt with him only in an impersonal way. It was management's attempt to be businesslike that in Mayo's opinion, led to the feelings of futility, which in turn caused the informal groups to develop. These groups were by no means an insignificant phenomenon. They had been observed in many companies, and managements had usually regarded them as unhealthy and conspiratorial. Sometimes they were thought of as precursors of eventual unionization, which indeed they sometimes were; more often they were considered to be the sources of attempt to deliberately restrict production. Mayo's research was the first to reveal in detail *from the inside* how and why these groups actually did accomplish this restriction.

Workers who found themselves assigned to the same work group were likely to discover that they had two things in common. There was for one thing a feeling of profound insignificance that was reinforced by the relative neglect with which they were treated. Poor work drew reprimands and threats, but good work was taken for granted and the paymaster's envelope was deemed reward enough for whatever contribution the individual had made. Common also was a resentment of management, sometimes because of shameful treatment but more often because of the lack of interest in or appreciation of the workers as individuals. Thus the bonds that held these groups together were based on the discovery of a mutual antagonism toward management. It is scarcely any wonder then, that one of the principal functions of the group was to provide a safe form of retaliation. This was done by tacit agreements that certain production volumes would not be exceeded, either individually or by sections. In those rare cases when an individual did not want to cooperate, he was ostracized. This left him completely alone, which was nearly intolerable for most workers. It was therefore a highly effective sanction for keeping any would-be mavericks in line. In addition to concealing the limitation of output by its members, the group offered other psychological rewards. One was an added feeling of security, since as long as productivity remained low, management was unlikely to either lay off workers or reduce their rate of pay. Another was a certain impish delight in deceiving the supervisors and their sophisticated allies, the efficiency engineers. Ironically, the workers were much more likely to be exhilarated by a successful battle of wits with the "stopwatch boys" than by anything that their jobs themselves could offer.

Mayo felt that there was a way out of this unproductive and mutually punitive relationship between managers and employees. The experiments with lighting and with rest periods had shown that under certain psychological conditions, the informal groups could actually become a very positive force for enhancing productivity. The key was to provide the workers with a sense of dignity and a sense of being appreciated. This was to be done by selecting as supervisors men who were inherently interested in and sensitive to people, and by training them to demonstrate a continuing personal interest in each employee.

We have already noted that it is naive to assume that human relations can be reduced to a simple matter of seeing to it that people in a position of authority treat their subordinates decently. To Mayo's credit, he and his associates foresaw the dangers of oversimplifying human relations, and they warned against assuming that supervisory

training, even if it were effective, would be a panacea. Unfortunately, their warnings went unheeded in a general gushing forth of enthusiasm for solving human relations problems. The results of the Hawthorne study had come at the right time: all of the historic forces that had been building management's susceptibility to an appeal for dealing more sympathetically with the employee had reached a peak. The rush was on. It was quickly discovered that there was indeed a market for solutions to human relations problems—even more so for simplistic formulas masquerading as solutions. Human relations problems were everywhere thrusting themselves upon management, either because their importance was at last realized or because of labor union pressures. These problems were vexing, unending, and frustrating. Management reached thirstily for panaceas, and these came forth abundantly.

There has been an enormous variety of what might be called fads in human relations. These have taken the form of articles, training courses, consulting services—indeed, even writers of books on the subject have not been immune to the temptation of offering glib advice. Although they vary somewhat in content, the simplified approaches to human relations have four things in common. First, they prescribe a set of rituals—things to do or say—that will presumably melt all resistance and dissolve all suspicion. Second, their underlying rationale, if any, is a brief list of supposedly instinctual needs to which all men are heir, and which, if satisfied, will render everyone cheerful and cooperative. Third, they are seldom if ever based on research but rather on the enthusiasm of their proponents or on self-evident logic. Fourth, they are usually harmless and sometimes moderately effective for a while, which wins them satisfied customers who become the most effective salesmen that fads could possibly expect.

All this prescribing, selling, and advocating has of course brought forth a series of reactions. Among social critics and certain business writers, the fads that pass for human relations have evoked derision. Thus there is jeering at the cults of "the happiness boys," and sometimes there is advocacy of an altogether objective, tough-minded approach to management. Among psychologists and sociologists, there are hand wringing and solemn warnings to students against being duped by charlatans. There are also, as we shall see presently, some very sophisticated research studies which illuminate the problems of human relations much more than Mayo was able to do. Among managers themselves, there is still a variety of reactions: there is the skepticism of the unconvinced, the zeal of the convert, and the

sadness of the disullusioned. There is also an important and growing number of managers who fully realize that the problems of human relations are considerably tougher to solve than the faddists have portrayed them to be.

Certainly Mayo and the reputable social researchers who followed him cannot be held responsible for human relations fads. Mayo provided the occasion, rather than the cause, for their emergence. In the last analysis, the durability of human relations fads can be traced to nothing more sinister than a desire for straightforward solutions and a failure to recognize that the problems involved were vastly more complex than they appeared to be. The measure of that complexity is the fact that those who have devoted their careers to analyzing human relations problems are still discovering new twists and subtleties. Indeed, the effects of the fads have not been altogether unfortunate. They have certainly helped to focus attention on the relationship of the individual worker and his supervisor. If that relationship is only a part of the total human relations context, it is nonetheless a vitally important part. It represents the best available channel for that two-way exchange of information that makes high morale possible: (1) making management's goals intelligible to the worker, and (2) making the worker's attitudes clear to management. It is also the indispensible link through which the organization is able to deliver whatever recognition it can to the individual. Above all, it is the best medium through which the company can foster the growth of its employees, which in the long run is probably the best guarantee of both morale and productivity.

What Happened at Prudential

Shortly after World War II, a group of social scientists at the University of Michigan formed an organization for the purpose of discovering and applying those principles of leadership that were associated with the highest productivity. This group eventually became known as the Institute for Social Research. Although their studies have branched out into several fields, that part of it which concerns us here was essentially an extension and refinement of Mayo's work. The Michigan researchers have followed Mayo's leads both broadly and deeply: broadly in the sense of having investigated the employee-supervisor relationship in a wide variety of work settings, and deeply in the sense of more sophisticated research techniques and a more searching analysis of cause and effect.

One of the earliest studies of the Michigan group is probably their best known. It was conducted among several large clerical departments at the headquarters of the Prudential Insurance Company of America in Newark shortly after World War II. The object of this study was to identify the supervisory styles of the men in charge of these departments and to determine what effect, if any, these styles had on the productivity of each department. Supervisory styles apparently do exist. Although it is true that a supervisor's overt tactics may change, or at least be perceived differently by different people, *his own concept of his job* tends to remain fairly constant. It was the relative constancy of this assumed or implicit job description that enabled the Michigan researchers to work out a feasible way to rate supervisory styles. In essence, they asked each supervisor to describe his job in his own words, tell what his objectives were, tell what obstacles stood in the way, and discuss what methods he preferred for reaching those objectives.

Based on what the supervisors themselves had to say, the Michigan researchers were able to divide them into three groups: those who were predominantly *production-centered,* those who were predominantly *employee-centered,* and those who displayed a mixed pattern. The word *predominantly* is important here because most supervisors have some of the characteristics of both groups, and the distinction made between them was based on broad trends rather than clearcut differences. (There are very few sharp distinctions between people in real life, and therefore the social researcher has to deal with approximations of the variable he is studying rather than with pure types.) A supervisor was considered production-centered if he felt that the main responsibility for getting the department's work done rested squarely on his own shoulders and that the function of his subordinates was to do his bidding so that it would get done. The supervisor made all decisions, issued instructions, and followed up continuously to ensure that these were carried out. Note that his *manner* was not crucial: he could have been pleasant or unpleasant. What mattered was his presumption that he was fully responsible and his subordinates were to do only what he told them to do.

A supervisor was considered employee-centered if he felt that in the last analysis it was his subordinates who actually got the work done, and that therefore they should also have the major responsibility for deciding *how* it should be done. The supervisor's role was not to direct but to coordinate: he provided needed information and materials, clarified the problems to be dealt with, and above all he strove

to maintain a friendly and harmonious atmosphere. Once again, the way in which he went about this was not as important as his intentions. He was trying to create conditions in which the employees themselves would find it easy to exercise responsibility for their own work.

The traditional management viewpoint was that work got done because a manager saw to it that it was done, and that lax or permissive supervision was an invitation to carelessness or soldiering. In that sense, the production-centered supervisors were carrying our management's wishes far more directly than were the employee-centered supervisors. But the research results were paradoxical, because there was a statistically significant tendency for the employee-centered supervisors to be in charge of highly productive groups and for production-centered supervisors to be in charge of less productive groups. (*Statistical significance* refers to a difference so great that it cannot be plausibly written off as a mere quirk of chance.) Obviously these results demanded reconsideration of long-accepted assumptions. Apparently too much management control could be self-defeating, and under certain conditions it seemed preferable to replace control with support. To make sense of their findings, the Michigan researchers had to make a somewhat radical assumption: many workers *liked* their jobs, *wanted* to be productive, and would be if they were given a significant share of *personal control* over their own jobs. If that assumption is granted, the results of the Prudential study are easy to explain. Yet the assumption is so contrary to traditional management thinking that it is still highly controversial.

Subsequent research has thrown new light on the controversy. The findings at Prudential were not peculiar to that company—or even to clerical functions in general—by any means. Very similar findings have turned up a wide variety of jobs, companies, and industrial settings. The theory that workers feel responsible for productivity, and that employee-centered supervision is the best way to stimulate this feeling, has plenty of research evidence to support it. It is also clear that employee-centered supervision is no panacea, and that at least three factors have an important influence on whether it helps or harms productivity: the extent to which the job requires teamwork; the consistency of the supervisor's behavior; and the personalities of the workers themselves. When work is so organized that the employees are highly interdependent and production depends on their ability to mesh their efforts smoothly, employee-centered supervision seems to pay off. Some examples of this type of work are crews

of airplanes, trains, or ships and most clerical operations. The effect of employee-centered supervision in such settings is to encourage the development of a team feeling or a "we" feeling; that is, the individual employees can derive a measure of pride from being part of a harmonious and effective group. Thus Mayo's prescription is fulfilled, and the inhibitions which production-centered supervision can bring— such as disinterest, resentment and fear of reprisal—are unlikely to come into play.

On the other hand, when the work must get done by individuals who have little if any interaction with their co-workers, employee-centered supervision is not necessarily an advantage and may even be a handicap. Trucking, crafts of all kinds, and certain types of "driver salesmen" such as milkmen and taxi drivers, fall into this category. The effect of employee-centered supervision in such cases is to create uncertainties as to what goals should be attained, whether one's performance has been satisfactory, and which of several alternative courses of action would be preferred by management. In this sense we can see that the effective supervisor must do much more than just encourage and coach; he must also be a reliable source of useful information. He must know how to give orders: not necessarily imperiously or with any suggestion of condescension, but clearly, pertinently and unmistakably. The worker whose colleagues do not provide him with a clear indication of what to do next must turn to the supervisor for further instructions, and if the supervisor is unable to indicate what is expected, the worker and his colleagues may well become demoralized. The demand for supportive supervision is greater, therefore, when the job itself does not provide informative feedback on the quality of one's performance than when it does.

We have already noted that there are very few supervisors whose style can be considered as a pure example of either approach. Most supervisors learn to adopt a mixed style that blends elements of both employee- and production-centered methods. Indeed, the Michigan researchers have come to regard a mixed style as optimum. The theoretically best approach adapts itself continuously to the demands of the job, the needs of the men being supervised, and the capabilities of the supervisor himself. It is, in other words, a continually evolving creative synthesis that provides whatever guidance, feedback, and support the men need to be fully productive under varying circumstances. A mixed style in itself is not necessarily conducive to productivity: what matters is how well the style can be adapted to different circumstances and personalities. A mixed style that is unresponsive to

these differences will have only random success; it will be appropriate some of the time and inappropriate at other times, probably without it ever being clear why the results are so variable. A supervisor who adheres rigidly to any style is likely to conclude that people are utterly unpredictable and that there is nothing he can do to affect their performance one way or another. However, to say that a supervisory style should be adaptable does not imply that it can be inconsistent or merely changeable. For example, some research conducted by the General Electric Company in one of its plants seemed to show that inconsistent supervisors—those who tried to follow a correct (employee-centered) style that they had been taught but who lapsed frequently into their "natural" styles—only succeeded in confusing and worrying their men.

How can a supervisor be both adaptable and consistent? Is it possible for him to be responsive to his subordinates and steadfast in his pursuit of organizational goals? To do this he would have to maintain a very delicate balance, and it is precisely for this reason that so few supervisors are truly masters of their jobs. What is perhaps not so obvious is that there is no inherent incompatibility between sensitivity to employees' needs and running a profitable operation. Therefore the delicate balance we are seeking, while it may be difficult, is by no means impossible. We will return to the latter point shortly when we discuss Rensis Likert's theories of management.

The apparent conflict between adaptability and consistency disappears when we analyze just what it is that the supervisor should be consistent with. Clearly, it cannot be any arbitrary set of rules or supposedly universal guidelines to effective supervision. Rather, *he has to be consistent with his own estimate of his men.* He can neither demand more of them than he feels they can produce nor settle for less than the best he knows they are capable of. He must challenge them without exhausting them, guide them without dominating them, help them without doing their work for them. In a word, he must know his men well and demonstrate this continually by the way he treats them. When he varies his tactics—when he becomes more or less permissive, more or less demanding—it must be because the job to be done requires it and not because he is experimenting or yielding to a whim. He should always be no less permissive than he can be and no more demanding than he must be. It does not really matter very much whether he manages to be ingratiating or whether he does not seem particularly friendly, since pleasantness in a supervisor is only a lubricant and unpleasantness only an irritant.

What does matter, and matters greatly, is whether the supervisor's appraisal of the abilities and reliability of his subordinates is reasonably accurate. If it is, and if he consistently provides them with the appropriate balance of direction and freedom, he will be showing his *respect for their individuality* in the most meaningful way. However, if he overestimates their capacities he may inflate their egos, and if he underestimates them he risks insulting them; worst of all, if he is sometimes aware of their capacities and sometimes ignores them, they are likely to conclude that he is not to be trusted. Supervisory style is therefore more a matter of how well a supervisor knows his men than of how adroitly he deals with them. Very often, badly mismanaged groups are victims of their supervisors' inability to appraise them correctly. Lax, inefficient groups may get that way because a supervisor assumes that strong guidance is not really necessary. Sullen, uncooperative groups may develop because a supervisor does not grant them the leeway they feel they deserve.

Finally, research has shown that the personality of the subordinates is a large factor in deciding under which supervisory style they would work best. Personality is an extremely important concept that is quite difficult to define. For our purposes, it should be understood as an individual's habitual ways of thinking about himself in relation to other people. Thus we might say that someone had a *dependent* personality if he tended to consider himself as relatively helpless and in need of protection from benefactors; he had an *independent* personality if he felt quite able to decide for himself what was in his best interests to do, and then to do it. Classifications of personality types such as this are convenient, but they should never be mistaken for the real dimensions from which personalities are constructed.

What we have described here as the independent type of person seems to work best under employee-centered supervision. This has been very clearly demonstrated in the case of research and development workers. Not all of these have independent personalities, of course, but the field tends to attract people with inquiring minds, people who do not take the conventional for granted and who take special pleasure in teaching themselves rather than in simply learning from precedent. When these people began to enter industry in large numbers shortly after the second world war, there was considerable consternation about their resentment of the normal rules of employee conduct and their seeming insistence on having rules of their own. Gradually it was realized that the research worker was for more productive when he was given a goal to work toward and left alone to

get there himself. Somewhat later, as the results of the Michigan studies and other social research studies began to accumulate, the realization grew that the advantages of "management by objectives" were not confined to the scientific type of employee. Managerial and professional workers in general, as well as any workers who happen to have a highly independent turn of mind, prefer to manage their own jobs to the maximum extent possible and are much more productive when permitted to do so than when they are closely controlled.

On the other hand, what we have called the dependent type of person is perhaps more numerous than the independent type and at any rate constitutes a large and significant part of the labor force. Included here are many young workers who may become independent later but begin their careers without a clearcut idea of their own capacties. Also included are older workers who have lived with production-centered supervision for many years and have grown accustomed to it and others whose experiences in life have taught them not to regard their own judgment too highly but to defer instead to tradition or to persons in authority. In general, it does not appear that employee-centered supervision has much of an effect on this type of person. Sometimes it causes the employee to wonder whether the supervisor really knows what the organization wants or to regard the supervisor as a rather pitiful caricature of what a real leader should be like. Being given an opportunity to set his own course does not inspire this sort of person to greater effort. Instead he will cast about for a more certain guide than his supervisor and will usually manage to find it in simple conformity to the habits, pace, and ideas of his peers. He is likely to feel more secure, and therefore to be more steadily productive, under the firm leadership of a production-centered supervisor whose style provides continual feedback as to what should and should not be done.

The Likert Theory

Most of the research that has been done by the Michigan group has been summarized and interpreted by Rensis Likert, one of the founders of the Institute for Social Research. His book, already regarded as a management classic, is required reading for any student who expects to specialize in human relations (3). Rather than attempt to summarize it here, we will simply highlight four themes that are particularly relevant to our consideration of supervisory styles.

First, Likert firmly rejects the idea that a serious concern for

good human relations is a distraction from the main business of management or that it is somehow incompatible with profitable operations. A clearheaded view of management, he maintains, requires us to realize that the main business of management is not to oversee or to control but rather to ensure the profitable use of the company's resources. Management control is only a means to an end rather than an end in itself, and, research has shown that there are many situations in which control per se is not the most effective way of achieving profitable operations. Instead of enforcing a uniformly production-centered and controlling form of management throughout an organization, management should analyze each of its operations and ensure that the particular style of supervision being utilized there is most conducive to sustained high productivity.

Second, Likert holds a great deal more than just sentiment or do-goodism is involved in management's attention to human relations. Profits are involved. Research has consistently shown that when supervisory style is attuned to the needs of the employees and the requirements of the job, productivity is significantly higher than when it is not. This refers, of course, only to jobs that are susceptible to worker-induced variation in productivity rates. Machine-paced jobs and those that are heavily dependent on external circumstances, such as retail sales, are obvious exceptions. But even when productivity advantages cannot be measured quantitatively, there is good reason to believe that appropriate supervision pays off. Workers' confidential reports on the degree of care and ingenuity they put into their work, as well as of the extent to which they conspire to limit production, all seem to bear a close relationship to whether they regard their supervision as helpful or oppressive.

Note that we are stressing appropriate supervision rather than making a blanket prescription for employee-centered styles. Likert is careful to note that employee-centered methods are not a theoretically based prescription but rather a *description* of the methods that have been adopted (usually instinctively) by the supervisors of most of the highly productive groups he has studied. We have already noted, however, that a sophisticated interpretation of employee-centered supervision stresses its adaptability and its adherence to a consistent appreciation of what the particular employees want and need rather than a doctrinaire insistence on being permissive.

Third, Likert stresses sustained productivity. In the last analysis this counts for far more than brief spurts of production, however spectacular these might be. Likert concedes the point that by apply-

ing heavy pressure, threats, and constant watchfulness, management can produce short-term productivity gains that are at least as great as those that accompany employee-centered methods. But this tactic bears the seeds of its own destruction. It nearly always causes a serious erosion of morale, which leads to turnover, inability to attract suitable new employees, restriction of output, strikes, and slow adaption to new methods. Pressure and control may be short-term expedients, but they should be reserved for emergency use only. They are hardly appropriate tactics for building continuously high morale and productivity.

Fourth, Likert cites the research evidence that shows that a responsible attitude toward one's work is a natural and widespread phenomenon. The main reason why it is not seen more often is that unwise supervisory tactics can easily dampen it or even suppress it altogether. This wellspring of responsibility can be tapped by supervision that treats workers with a clear respect for their trustworthiness, realism, and commonsense. It does very little good to seek to develop this sense of "proprietorship" over one's job by exhortation. You cannot merely tell a man that you respect him and expect him to behave as if he believed you. As we shall see in greater detail in Chapter Five, employees pay attention to a great deal more than just what is said in forming their opinions of their company. In fact, since formal statements are more susceptible to dissimulation, or at least to purely momentary bursts of sincerity, they are probably regarded less seriously by employees than any other manifestation of management's intentions.

What counts, of course, is not words but action. The most convincing action that management can take to demonstrate its respect for the employee's ability to be responsible for his own work is to let him control it. This means more than merely minimizing the amount of instructions he receives and the number of records and rules that are used to control his activities. It means consulting him about matters which affect the day-to-day flow of his work. It means advising him of matters that affect the background of his work, so that even if he is unable to use this information for his own decisions he will have a better understanding of management's decisions. This means taking the employee into partnership with management: not a partnership of ownership, but one of participation in the planning that directly affects the employee's job.

There was a time when management could say that what the employee didn't know wouldn't hurt him, and that in any case he only

wanted to know what to do and what he'd be paid for doing it. Today we know that we can no longer afford to be complacent about sharing information and at least some degree of decision-making responsibility with employees. By inviting employees to participate in a limited way in activites that were, traditionally, the exclusive province of management, we can encourage whatever natural tendencies they have to accept responsibility for their own work. This is apparently the only secret of those supervisors whose departments have turned in consistently superior performance records.

Management Philosophies

Social research in industry seems to imply that the assumptions that managers make about their jobs and their subordinates have a more important effect on human relations than the overt things they do and say. It is well worth examining the validity of these assumption in some detail.

One thing that we are likely to discover when we examine any particular manager's assumptions is his insistence that he hasn't made any. Most managers are pragmatic, matter-of-fact men who handle problems as they arise. He does very little theorizing about what concepts can account for his experience or what generalized forces may underlie the problems he encounters. But he probably has certain ideas that he does not question and cannot prove; he probably takes for granted certain ideas that he may have never examined seriously at all. A clearcut understanding of these ideas can emerge only after a careful analysis is made of why he handles his job the way he does. Without such an analysis, these concepts tend to blend too easily with the normal background of his thought for him to notice them. These "ideas," which are not ideas at all in the conscious sense, but missing

links in the mental processes that tie his actions to his past experiences, are what we mean by assumptions. To have such assumptions is by no means a peculiarity of managers. Everyone has them. On balance, they are very useful: obviously, very little would get done if every untested assumption had to be dredged up, evaluated, and either certified as valid or discarded. Assumptions are extremely economical, especially when they fit the facts.

Obviously, statements of corporate policy regarding human relations cannot be taken as a literal prescription of how people in that corporation shall be treated. But neither are they mere oratory. Rather, they represent the directions in which the company wishes to go and the yardsticks by which it will measure its own actions toward its employees. We have drawn a distinction here between the explicit assumptions a company makes regarding people—that can be found in its formal corporate credo or objectives or found in the public statements of its leading executives—and its implicit assumptions—that can be deduced from the characteristic ways in which its relationships with its employees are actually handled. For practical purposes, it is far more important to know what implicit assumptions govern these relationships. However, explicit credos can have a significant impact on the human relations practices of a company, *provided* they are based on a realistic appraisal of what the company's employees actually need to derive from their jobs, and also provided that the company makes a serious effort to discover and examine its implicit assumptions and to modify them wherever they vary substantially with the company's explicit credo.

Later in this chapter we will examine several explicit credos that have been, on the whole, quite effective in guiding the human relations practices of leading companies. But first it will be necessary to consider implicit assumptions in more detail. For this purpose, we will briefly review the theories of Chris Argyris and the late Douglas McGregor, two leading analysts of implicit management philosophies and their impacts on human relations.

The Argyris Analysis

Argyris begins his analysis of management's traditional assumptions by noting that the ordinary worker is considered to have very little self-discipline or personal pride; if he thinks for himself at all, the resulting ideas are likely to be short-sighted and foolish. If management really assumes such things about the average worker, then

clearly their ideas are badly in need of being brought up to date. Yet Argyris often seems able to make the charge stick. What other reason can be given for the widespread use of highly directive, controlling styles of supervision?

In another study of Argyris's work, the following interpretation is made of one of his main themes:

Most organizations, especially at the lower levels, are geared for men who make a very child-like adjustment to life: They leave very little leeway for choosing, for using discretion, or for adapting rules to fit circumstances. Most employees are expected to do just as they are told and leave the thinking to the foreman, whose capacity for doing so is a perennially moot point among the people he supervises. In any case millions of grown men are required to spend forty hours a week suppressing their brainpower in order to maintain a system that is not nearly as efficient as it looks. (4:73)

The assumptions about workers that may be deduced from a great deal of traditional management activity is not, in other words, nearly as complimentary toward those workers as many overt credos and statements of corporate philosophy would have it. Employees react to management's behavior and not to its protestations. The grown man who finds his adulthood unrecognized in the course of his employment may rebel, leave, or submit as he wishes; none of these alternatives permit him to reach whatever heights of productivity of which he might be capable—not in *that* company, at any rate.

This indeed is Argyris' main point. He does not like to see ambitions frustrated and dignity ignored, but he likes even less to see an organization that is prevented by its own mythology from running itself to its own best advantage. He concedes that some employees—perhaps even a sizable number—are less mature than one might hope, but he insists that there are enormous reserves of untapped maturity in the labor force that could respond to more realistic supervision with a significant outpouring of effort. What is this maturity that traditional management philosophy assumes to be in chronically short supply and that Argyris insists is far more widely distributed than many managers would dare to believe? It is not, of course, solely a matter of age. Rather it has a great deal to do with the extent to which an individual has profited from his experiences in life: with the extent to which he has learned realism, self-control, and emotional independence. Maturity is not really a stage one reaches but rather a direction in which one progresses through life—if he progresses at all.

In outlining the distinction between the mature and immature individual, Argyris notes seven major trends or processes that normally

occur as the child grows into a man and as the man grows into an increasingly capable and effective adult. These trends are essentially recapitulations of the observations of many psychologists, and in citing them Argyris is simply giving special stress to those processes that traditional management assumptions hardly credit with occurring at all. Argyris is saying, in other words, that the traditional management theories fly in the face of what is known about human psychological development because they assume that this development is usually arrested shortly after it starts.

The seven processes cited by Argyris are: first, that whereas a child is relatively passive, an adult is relatively active. The child needs to be stimulated or disciplined or given some signal by the environment as to what he should do. The adult draws his own conclusions as to what the environment requires of him, and can initiate his own action. *He does not, in other words, need a supervisor to control his actions, any more than he needs a parent to control him. What he needs is a clear indication of what is required of him, and why. A mature adult will take care of the rest.*

Second, whereas a child is relatively dependent, an adult is relatively independent. The child needs to be reassured by the presence of the adults on whom he depends, or at least by familiar sights and sounds. Lacking a clearcut notion of what is right or wrong, wise or foolish, he tends to conform to the actions and attitudes of his peers. On the other hand, the adult is usually able to develop his own interests and values and can cling to them even in the face of severe pressure to conform. He may find individualism uncomfortable, but if the principle in question means enough to him, he can abandon comfort. *He is not, in other words, willing to sacrifice everything for the sake of preserving his employment. If his pride or his sense of justice are challenged, he may be quite willing to risk everything—his job included —to defend them.*

Third, whereas the child is usually able to respond to a given situation in a limited number of ways, the adult is capable of responding in a wide variety of ways. Indeed, the adult prefers to vary his methods and his style from time to time; he does not like to be turned by repetition and habit into an automaton. *He does not need to be shown the one, best way to do a job. He will become bored if he repeats any set of actions without variation, and variation may actually result in higher productivity than the best method used* ad infinitum.

Fourth, whereas a child has a rather short attention span, the adult

is capable of a deep and abiding interest in a number of subjects. The child's enthusiasms are brief and he may forget a topic that engrossed him shortly after he is distracted from it. The adult's curiosity and inventiveness may be engaged by almost any material with which he frequently comes into contact. *He may not, in other words, regard this work as simply a routine to be endured, but rather as a challenge to his skill and creativity.*

Fifth, whereas the child's time perspective is quite short, the adult's is quite long. The adult has a memory and does not lightly ignore the lessons he has learned in the past. Therefore, it is no simple matter to recapture his loyalty once it is lost or to break him away from beliefs he has cherished for a long while. He is not easily distracted or dazzled. He regards inconsistency with cynicism and changes his mind slowly if at all. *There are, in other words, no easy tricks by which the management can undo their mistakes of the past. Similarly, the adult anticipates the future and can postpone current satisfactions to enhance the probability of greater satisfactions in the future. He is capable of making sacrifices if it appears to be worth his while to do so.*

Sixth, whereas the child is usually subordinate to everyone, the adult can play both subordinate and superior roles. He is not a prisoner of either role and usually accepts someone else's leadership as legitimate only if it appears necessary and only if that individual can earn his respect as a leader. *The adult does not enjoy being told exactly what to do and when to do it. Being bossed is often a burden to him rather than a comforting indication of what must be done.*

Seventh, whereas the child has only a relatively vague notion of who he is, the adult is acutely aware of his individuality and may be painfully sensitive to anything that appears to diminish his feelings of self-worth. *The adult cannot be taken for granted. He cannot simply be given a place to work, materials to work on, and someone to see that he does the work. He must also be given information, encouragement, recognition, and challenge. His ego comes to work with him, and it must be reckoned with.*

We might summarize these seven trends by saying that the typical adult is considerably more subtle, more noble, more complex, and more adaptable than he has sometimes been assumed to be. But what kind of environment is this adult likely to encounter in industry, and how well does it meet his needs? Argyris notes three major aspects of the industrial environment that he considers decidedly *inappropriate* for mature adults but that are nevertheless quite wide-

spread and deeply rooted in tradition. They are formal organization structure, directive styles of leadership, and management controls.

The organization structure of industry typically concentrates decision-making power at the top, with each level of management holding onto a sizable part of whatever trickles down to them. At the level of the individual worker, the leeway left for making decisions is negligible. Argyris feels that this eventually has a stultifying effect on whatever interest and enthusiasm the individual might once have possessed. Industry is of course aware of this problem and has developed a widespread use of decentralization. But decentralized decision-making is easier to plan than to carry out: a failure at any level to delegate sufficient authority downwards dams up the process all the way down the line.

We have already dealt with directive styles of leadership at length: this is Argyris' term for what we have referred to in Chapter Three as production-centered supervision. Suffice it to say that leadership that reserves unto itself too many of the decisions that mature adults are perfectly capable of making for themselves is scarcely likely to maintain effective morale.

By management controls Argyris refers to budgets, schedules, production quotas, and all forms of measurement that have the effect of maintaining a form of scrutiny over the individual's performance. The problem lies not so much with the existence of targets (which if realistically set can be effective incentives), as with the way in which they tend to be administered. Too often, the measurement becomes an end in itself that narrows management's perspective to short-range, partial goals. As a result, the individual employee is also taught to concentrate on "looking good on paper," which usually means conformity to a prescribed way of doing his job and suppressing whatever imagination he might otherwise have brought to bear.

Admittedly Argyris paints a gloomy picture, and the realities of industrial life are not always quite so bleak as the foregoing paragraphs might suggest. Argyris would be the first to concede that in analyzing what is wrong with industry he has had to concentrate on the sources of its malfunctions. He has thus given relatively little attention to industry's own efforts at self-correction. To his credit, he has also made an exhaustive study of what might be done to improve the situation he has described. While this is a rather complex prescription, it has two essential features. First, he advocates a deliberate cultivation of flexibility by all organizations. That is, they should consciously vary their leadership styles and control structure to suit the

varying demands that are made upon them from time to time. Such a process of changing must be carried out with great delicacy and speed and would require a degree of mutual confidence and a level of communications very nearly unheard of in most organizations.

His second recommendation, therefore, is that the interpersonal processes of a company—the ability of its management and employees to make their purposes intelligible to each other—be strengthened through sensitivity training. This is a process in which key personnel are taught to understand their personal impact on others and to elimi-nate unintentional barriers to effective communication.

The McGregor Analysis

Douglas McGregor's work is important both as a recapitulation of what most social research in industry seems to imply and as a use-ful analytic tool in its own right. He made the by-now famous distinc-tion between theories X and Y, which are simply labels for des-ignating contrasting management assumptions without implying any prejudgment as to which is better. However, McGregor made it quite clear that some assumptions are preferable to others; not because some are always right and others always wrong, but rather because the circumstances under which companies must operate vary. The best assumptions are fitted as realistically as possible to the actual circum-stances of the particular company, rather than applied uncritically as eternal verities whose applicability is not to be questioned. He also advocated freeing the individual from unnecessary restrictions, not because the individual will necessarily like this, but because it is like-ly to make him more productive.

McGregor found that unrealistic assumptions about people were at the bottom of many a carefully planned, expensively implemented failure. When a plan unwittingly flies in the face of human nature, its success can be no greater than the extent to which it can be carried out without people. Unfortunately, the failure of many such plans is frequently attributed to uncooperativeness on the part of the people who were to have put them into effect. The usual prescription is for tighter controls over them. McGregor held that very often it was ex-cessive control that provoked the uncooperativeness in the first place and that tightened controls only aggravate the situation.

Theory X is a rather pessimistic and unflattering assessment of the average worker but one which continues to be regarded as hard-headed realism in many quarters. That it is hardheaded can scarcely

be doubted, but whether it is realistic very often is open to question. Theory X is essentially based on these three basic assumptions: (1) Work is neither a natural nor a congenial activity for the average man. Given the choice, he would prefer to do almost anything else. (2) This average man must be compelled to work. It must be a matter of survival, and the threat of dismissal or of other sanctions must be employed to ensure that he will not indulge his natural penchant for not working. (3) If he must work, this average man would at any rate prefer not to think. Analyzing and making decisions are hardly more congenial to him than work itself; he must therefore, be given detailed and continuing guidance as to what to do. Theory X might be summarized as assuming that most people are lazy, lacking in self-control, and unable to think for themselves. Presented in this way, it almost seems like a caricature of what a reasonable manager would be willing to believe. But this is chiefly because it is so inconsistent with our prevailing national ethic. Many operating plans, when stripped of their rationalizations, really boil down to very little more than theory X.

On the other hand, theory Y is not the diametric opposite of theory X, and neither is it a prescription of indiscriminate sympathy or patience with the worker. It is built on these four basic assumptions: (1) Work is neither inherently attractive nor unattractive; rather each man develops an attitude toward work that is the result of his experience with it. If he dislikes work it is because he has learned to dislike it; thus, it is also possible for him to learn to like it. (2) While the authoritarian, controlling methods implied by theory X can lead to profitable operating results, they are not the only means of doing so. Indeed, there are other methods that may, under certain circumstances, be considerably more efficient. Further, supervisory methods that stress control can lead to side effects that weaken the company's ability to continue to operate profitably. In other words, the value of applying theory X to management must be measured in terms of *all* of its results and not in terms of short-run production. When this is done, theory X emerges as an approach of limited applicability that is used much more often than is optimum. (3) Most people can select goals for themselves, and once having done so they pursue those goals with as much determination as they can. If the goal is their own— something they can recognize as congruent with their own basic needs—they will need no urging to pursue it. People can, in other words, *motivate themselves* quite apart from any external pressure. Such self-motivation is usually stronger and more lasting than any

motivation that can be imposed by management. The task of management is not to find tighter methods for control but to find ways of harmonizing the organization's goals with the individual's goals. (4) Most people have no inherent antipathy for responsibility. Many actually seek it as a more fulfilling and exhilarating experience than is afforded by most humdrum jobs. When a responsible attitude toward work is lacking, it may be due to the absence of any real decision-making control over the job rather than to disinterest or irresponsibility on the part of the worker.

Theory Y might be summarized as assuming that most people develop their attitudes toward work as a consequence of their experiences with it, and that they are capable of developing a quite mature and responsible attitude if they are treated like mature and responsible people. That is, they should be given the maximum opportunity to make their own decisions and to follow their own style of working. When it is necessary for them to conform to higher level decisions, they should be given an opportunity to discuss and understand the reasons why conformity is required. Theory Y does not altogether dismiss authoritarian methods of control, it merely proposes to use them only when they are necessary.

According to theory Y, the main task of management is to find ways of harmonizing the goals of management and the goals of the individual. There is no direct way to do this: You cannot persuade either to abandon its goals for the sake of the other. It is really more a matter of management making a clearer distinction between its goals and its methods for attaining them, and then being prepared to modify or even abandon some of those methods if better ways of reaching its goals can be found. One such method consists, essentially, of inviting nonmanagers to exercise as much control and responsibility as they care to; this of course implies management's readiness to surrender as much of its traditional authority as proves to be unnecessary. The greatest difficulty with theory Y lies, therefore, in requiring management not merely to recognize responsibility in nonmanagers (which, even if it comes as a revelation, is not terribly difficult) but also in requiring them to relinquish some authority. That is often hard to do because it is precisely the possession of authority—the power to make decisions—that makes management such a satisfying job for many managers. It may even be what attracted them to the managerial ranks in the first place. Theory Y clearly implies that managers are not alone in enjoying authority. Even though managers will con-

tinue to be the principal source of control in the organization, they should, according to this theory, seek to share at least some of that control with their subordinates.

Another difficulty with theory Y is that it demands innovation. There is no simple formula whereby it can be applied. (Given our experience with human relations fads, however, this may be a blessing in disguise.) Theory Y requires a continuing dialogue between a manager and his men in which their capacity for controlling their own work is continuously stimulated, tested and enlarged. More than mere delegation is involved. The manager must first develop a realistic appreciation of what each man can do and of how he would prefer to be treated, and then convey his willingness to deal with the man on his own terms (or at least to meet him halfway). What is required is more of an exchange of attitudes and of confidence than of promises or instructions. In other words, theory Y places a heavy burden on the manager's *interpersonal competence*. It does not permit him to be aloof or indifferent or defensive.

A third difficulty with theory Y is that it is not a complete answer to the problems of employee motivation. Of course it does not claim to be; but it is enough of a departure from traditional management thinking to cause some people to believe, erroneously, that it proposes to dispense with financial incentives and to solve all problems with artistry in human relations.

Actually the most powerful combination of incentives usually involves *both* meaningful financial rewards and an environment that encourages personal styles of working. High financial rewards in an unstimulating environment usually create skin-deep loyalty, cynicism, and an unwillingness to go beyond customary levels of exertion or care. Similarly, fascinating work which is poorly recompensed is likely to lead to disillusionment and high rates of turnover. Theory Y recognizes that most men have pecuniary drives but insists that these are not necessarily their strongest drives.

Theory Y is a formula that is not easy to apply. It demands more managerial skill, wisdom, and patience than theory X. But what it requires most of all is a point of view that keeps both organizational and individual goals in a frank, unemotional perspective. All management philosophies lead indirectly to whatever results they produce, and McGregor's theory Y would seem, on the basis of research evidence, to be more likely to bring about positive results than would theory X.

Three Explicit Philosophies

Managements are by no means unaware of the problems discussed by social researchers such as Argyris and McGregor. In fact, much of what they have to say might be considered a distillation and formalization of what has been apparent to sophisticated managers for some time. In recent years an excellent forum for the presentation of executive and corporate philosophies has been the annual McKinsey Foundation Lecture Series at Columbia University. I have chosen three of these lectures to illustrate explicit philosophies. Before presenting them, a few caveats are in order.

First, these three philosophies are not necessarily representative of industry at large. They were chosen simply because they are convenient, well stated, and represent well-known companies. Second, it is not suggested that any of these statements is necessarily an accurate portrayal of the quality of human relations throughout each of the vast corporations represented here. Rather they are presented, as suggested earlier, as indications of the directions in which the corporations would like to move regarding human relations and of the yardsticks with which they measure their own progress in those directions. Third, the analysis made of each selection is designed to highlight similarities and differences, rather than stand as a criticism. This is especially true since the remarks to be quoted are out of their original contexts and were written not for comparative purposes but as expressions of a particular corporate viewpoint.

Let us first consider some remarks by the then president of E. I. du Pont de Nemours and Company, Crawford H. Greenewalt. In his McKinsey Lectures, (5)* he gives particular stress to two ways of motivating superior performance on the part of men whose capacities are not necessarily superior—which he regards, incidentally, as one of the central tasks of corporate management. The first method consists essentially of what we have referred to as employee-centered supervision. But note the practical light in which Greenewalt views the *effects* of such supervision and his willingness to face the unpleasant but nevertheless realistic prospect of failure.

I suppose the difference between good management and bad management can be said to depend upon how it deals with this question of shared re-

---

* From *The Uncommon Man* by Crawford H. Greenewalt. Copyright © 1959, the Trustees of Columbia University. Used by permission of McGraw-Hill Book Company.

sponsibility [between a manager and a subordinate]. If a manager interprets his duties as requiring him to stand with his hand eternally on his subordinate's shoulder, he is a poor manager and his subordinate cannot possibly do his job well. The alternative, of course, is to give him every opportunity to do the job in his own way, with whatever general guidance is necessary. If he fails, one must admit to a bad initial choice and look for a better replacement.

These alternatives frequently leave one suspended between frying pan and fire. If a poor job is being done, there is always the temptation to step in and take over and, to some, this seems the more humane course. It takes far more courage to admit to a poor selection, but that recognition and the unpleasant replacement process is far better for the business, and, in the long run, kinder to the misplaced incumbent. Forbearance is indeed an essential managerial attribute, but it is useless if the courage is lacking to be tough-minded in recognizing and facing up to the deficiencies of the man who fails to click. (5:14)

This point of view might be summarized as requiring each man to rely on his own resources as much as possible, on the assumption that competence will be enhanced and incompetence will make itself apparent quickly enough to be eliminated before any great harm is done. This approach obviously relies heavily on management's ability to select competent people to fill key jobs. It should be noted that competence is, after all, a relative thing; many people may be in a process of evolving toward competence at a time when they are given heavy responsibilities. They should not be treated as errors in selection if coaching, demonstrations, and moral support from their managers can help them to grow quickly enough on the job. There is, in other words, a point beyond which a laissez-faire approach to management does no service to either the company or the individual.

The second major method cited by Greenewalt for motivating uncommonly good job performance is financial compensation. He states a more or less classical case for the efficacy of money as a motivator.

Of all the motivations to which the human mechanism responds . . . none has proved so powerful as that of financial gain. Although the Midas complex has long since become a rarity, self enrichment is a dream which must rank with the most compelling forces in shaping the destinies of the human race. It has always been so, and when we are disturbed over being members of a "materialistic generation," we can look back over history and note that we are simply expressing a basic human trait. . . .

The importance of a financial lure is not that the accumulation of wealth is in itself significant, but because money is the only form of incentive which is wholly negotiable, appealing to the widest possible range of seekers. As people differ so markedly, it is difficult if not impossible to

apply any other common denominator of inducement fully acceptable to all. Money was invented for the precise purpose of meeting widely dissimilar desires. (5:14)

It is the flexibility of money that makes it such a powerful motivator, especially when it operates in tandem with other motivators. However it should be noted in passing that the flexibility of money—its ability to satisfy a wide range of desires—is limited at lower income levels. When all of an income is committed to subsistence or to the accumulation of the material requirements for a better standard of living, not much choice is involved in how it is to be spent. The incentive effect of money that will be spent to pay the grocer and money that can be spent to satisfy one's heart's desire are two different things. This makes the administration of high level salaries considerably more complex than the job of setting hourly wages.

Next, consider the philosophy of General Electric Company as stated by its former president, Ralph J. Cordiner. In his McKinsey lectures (6)*, Cordiner stresses two other techniques for enhancing the productivity of employees: (1) clear delineation of responsibilities and (2) leadership by persuasion. In these passages, he makes a strong case for the scientific management approach, which proceeds from the assumption that it is management's basic job to make the production process entirely rational and to make its rationale completely clear to the people who must execute it:

Now, the President is of course unable to do all the work himself, and so he delegates the responsibility for portions of the total work through organization channels to individuals who have the talents and knowledge required to do it. This is done by planning and building the work of the company into an organization structure which consists of all the necessary positions and components required to do all the work in the most effective and efficient manner.

Each employee thus takes on responsibility for some part of the over-all company work. Along with this responsibility, each position naturally carries with it full accountability for measured results, and all the necessary authority required for the position except those authorities specifically stated as withheld. Therefore each employee of the company has, in his position, full responsibility, authority, and accountability for a certain defined body of work and teamwork. . . .

With this philosophy, General Electric achieves a community of purpose between leaders and their associates, and is able to attain that voluntary

---

* From *New Frontiers for Professional Managers* by Ralph J. Cordiner. Copyright © 1956, the Trustees of Columbia University. Used by Permission of McGraw-Hill Book Company.

integration which is the hallmark of a free and decentralized enterprise. (6:48)

This philosophy might be summarized by saying that if each man is given his own clearly defined bailiwick into which no one else is permitted to trespass, he will regard his job in much the same light as he might regard a possession. He will handle his job carefully and diligently. The confusion of too many bosses and of overlapping responsibilities is avoided. As in a well-trained army, each man has his job to do and knows what is expected of him. This is a highly rational approach in that it looks at an organization as a system of allocated responsibilities and reporting relationships. A more sentimental view might regard an organization as a collection of individuals, for each of whom the organization is only a part of their lives. Of course, every organization is both of these things—a formal system and a group of people—but too much emphasis on either aspect can injure the organization's efficiency.

Note the subtle difference between Greenewalt's approach and Cordiner's. Cordiner stresses defining where a man's responsibility begins and ends, while Greenewalt seems to prefer showing him where it begins and letting him discover for himself where it should end. Either approach if carried to an extreme could be damaging. Each, within reasonable limits, serves an important purpose. Both Cordiner and Greenewalt would undoubtedly agree that balance between the two viewpoints is the real key to good management.

Cordiner's second major point concerns leadership by persuasion. Notice that he consistently adheres to his basically rational point of view. His managerial philosophy is essentially a series of deductions from his fundamental premise, which is that the design of the organization must be based on analysis, and its logic must be made clear to everyone involved. Notice also how, like Greenewalt, he shows the businessman's realistic willingness to deal with failure should it occur.

. . . effective and flexible integration can be achieved through the formulation and communication of common objectives and policies, and common means for measurement, so that the man in the decentralized components of the organization will voluntarily and responsibly make sound decisions in the interests of the entire enterprise.

In this situation, the manager's work is to lead others by drawing out their ideas, their special knowledge, and their efforts. Since self-discipline rather than boss-discipline is the hallmark of a decentralized organization, the manager resorts to command only in emergencies where he must admit temporary failure to make the situation and the necessary course of

action self-evident. To the degree that the contributions of every individual are made voluntarily and are self-disciplined, the manager is leading
by persuasion rather than command. (6:75)

Although Cordiner does not define persuasion further, it is clear
that what he means by it is any action by which the manager makes
the company's goals intelligible and attractive to the worker. To the
extent that the manager tries to accomplish this through sheer sales-
manship, he is likely to find himself forced to fall back on his authority more often than he wishes. Even without the implied threat of
command, being "persuaded" often smacks too much of being treated
as an obstacle to be removed. It is far more effective and artful to accomplish persuasion by consulting with the men involved and by
working with them to formulate a joint plan of action.

We might contrast Cordiner's and Greenewalt's approaches by
saying that Cordiner would steer the company from the top by par-
celing out to each subordinate manager that piece of the total plan
that he is to administer. Greenewalt would prefer to orchestrate and
unify the various directions that result from the "steering" actions of
all of the various managers. The actual difference between these two
philosophies is probably much subtler than can be conveyed here. But
these subtleties help to form the fabric of human relations practices in
a company.

Finally, consider the point of view presented by Thomas J. Watson, Jr., chairman of International Business Machines Corporation, in
his McKinsey Lectures (7)*. To begin with, he acknowledges the importance of what we have referred to here as assumptions. He uses
the word *beliefs*, but aside from the difference between what is implicit and what is explicit, the terms have a very similar meaning. In
considering the practical importance of these assumptions, Watson
goes beyond the claims of social researchers such as Argyris and
McGregor. He attributes the major credit for a company's long-term
successes (or by implication, for its failures also) to its beliefs. Note
that he stresses the soundness of these beliefs, which is essentially a
matter of understanding the environment within which the company
operates; and adherence to these beliefs even when a changing environment demands that the company develop new strategies or tactics:

This, then, is my thesis: I firmly believe that any organization, in order
to survive and achieve success, must have a sound set of beliefs on which
it premises all its policies and actions.

* From *A Business and Its Beliefs* by Thomas J. Watson, Jr. Copyright ©
1964, the Trustees of Columbia University. Used by permission of McGraw-
Hill Book Company.

Next, I believe that the most important single factor in corporate success is faithful adherence to those beliefs.

And finally, I believe that if an organization is to meet the challenges of a changing world, it must be prepared to change everything about itself except those beliefs as it moves through corporate life. (7:5)

Of the beliefs that have guided the management of IBM, respect for the individual is the one Watson considers the most important. This is of course a common phrase, and its application in a particular company usually acquires a characteristic style or flavor that is not quite the same as in any other company.

As this next passage brings out, respect for the individual in IBM is intended to be an inclusive concept: it applies to everyone, and if anything it may even be somewhat weighted in favor of those employees who are not as well equipped (with money or authority) as are others. Respect for the individual in this context means protecting him from both economic insecurity and capricious management.

We go to great lengths to develop our people, to retrain them when job requirements change, and to give them another chance if we find them experiencing difficulties in the jobs they are in.

This does not mean that a job at IBM is a lifetime ticket or that we do not occasionally let people go—we do, but only after we have made a genuine effort to help them improve. . . .

Among plant people, where job security is ordinarily a matter of major concern, IBM's ability to avoid layoffs and work interruptions has encouraged our people to respond with loyalty and with diligence on the job. . .

Today our frequent attitude surveys show that the importance we attach to job security is one of the principle reasons why people like to work for IBM. (7:15)

What we referred to earlier as the "rational approach" taken by Cordiner—in which each man knows what he should do and management makes sure that he does it—is given relatively little emphasis by Watson. Instead the emphasis is on reassuring the individual that his employment will not be terminated (except in the extreme instances of incorrigibility or incompetence), and that his justifiable complaints will be heard. No one man in authority—or even several men—will block him from receiving a full hearing.

The emphasis is on reassurance, rather than on clearcut instructions and measurement. Watson notes that for years no detailed records of individual production were kept in IBM plants because the company preferred to base compensation on an over-all evaluation of the individual's work. Obviously, the underlying assumption is that when the individual is freed of the basic anxieties associated with em-

ployment, he will spontaneously and continuously do his best on the job.

Note the subtle differences between the approach to management taken by Greenewalt and that taken by Watson. Both afford the manager considerable latitude and expect to measure him by the results he obtains, but Watson also takes an interest in the *means* used to attain those results. He wants to be certain that no departmental goal is achieved at the expense of an employee's dignity or sense of fair play, because preserving that dignity is a higher corporate objective than any particular departmental goal.

Like all business philosophies, the chief strength of the IBM approach lies in its balanced application, and its chief weakness lies in the possibility of overemphasis. Too much stress on job security, for example, can lead to disinterest on the part of those employees to whom challenge is more important than security; too much countermanding of management's decisions can lead to forgetting the fact that managers have human relations problems of their own.

This brief review of explicit management philosophies has attempted to illustrate two main points: (1) the principles by which companies are consciously guided are seldom as outdated as theory X and often take cognizance in a practical way of advanced thinking and social research results; (2) these philosophies differ among themselves in subtle but important shadings of emphasis, and these shadings probably help to give each organization its own characteristic human relations climate.

Communication

So much has been said and written about the importance of an effective communication system in organizations that it almost seems redundant to make the point again. Unfortunately, communication is still an extremely important and frequently misunderstood phenomenon, and as organizations get larger it will very likely become an even more critical problem.

Communication, in the sense that we are using the term, may be thought of as any system by which people obtain information that affects the way in which they perform their jobs. Perhaps the most obvious comment to make at the outset is that communication actually consists of a great deal more than what individual managers say or information that managements publish. Corporations frequently overlook this obvious point when they attempt to improve their communications systems.

In one sense, an organization can be no more efficient than the system by which it informs its members of what is expected of them, so that their efforts will reinforce each other and create a momentum

toward the attainment of the organization's purpose. Any failure of communication is at best wasteful and at worst demoralizing.

Channels of Communication

There are three major communication channels within any organization: formal, informal, and implicit. These channels tend to operate simultaneously.

The *formal* channel includes any official, deliberate, overt statement made by managers to employees (collectively or individually) or vice versa. The formal channel includes everything that one party wants the other party to know. It is therefore calculated to make the sending party look good to the receiver, and for that very reason it tends to be at least partially discounted by the receiving party. Many attempts to improve communication actually consist of making the formal channels more palatable or more attractive. There is certainly nothing wrong with this, especially from an aesthetic standpoint. But it should come as no surprise when polished communications are no more convincing than unpolished ones, if their main purpose is to propagandize rather than to inform.

The *informal* channel consists of rumors, gossip, and speculation. It generally corresponds to what is commonly known as the grapevine. Sometimes the informal channels are erroneously regarded as competitor to the formal, and efforts are made to attract employees away from the informal sources. As we shall see, informal communication channels are natural and not necessarily unhealthy; they can serve as a useful adjunct to the formal channels and be an extremely sensitive barometer of morale. If the formal channels carry messages that the senders want the receivers to believe, then the informal channels carry messages that the senders themselves want to believe. More precisely, the informal channels reflect both the hopes and anxieties of the senders; their biases and value judgments. It is for this reason that informal communications, quite apart from whether or not they happen to be factual, carry diagnostic information of the greatest importance to anyone who would analyze what happens to information as it is transmitted through a company.

The *implicit* channel includes all of the unchallenged, taken-for-granted "folklore" of an organization, including its favorite myths about itself and the reasons for all of its traditions. This channel does not *convey* information so much as it *filters* it. That is, the implicit communications system within an organization determines what will

seem reasonable to members of that organization and what will seem incongruous. It affects the kinds of questions people feel free to ask and the question they regard as taboo.

We will discuss each channel more fully a little further on in this chapter, but it might be helpful to make some general observations first. The most important quality of any message in any channel is its *believability*. This is less a matter of its clarity or the skill with which it is sent than of its congruence with what is already believed. The formal statement that flies in the face of the prevalent rumor, or the speculation that cannot be reconciled with established traditions, tend to be greeted with suspicion or rejected altogether. The three channels normally fit together in a roughly consistent whole. Whatever is grossly inconsistent with what is already believed tends to be perceived more as a distracting noise than as a clear and pertinent bit of truth. This is why the most effective communications systems are those in which the formal messages are sent in cognizance of the informal and implicit channels. Those systems in which formal messages either ignore or try to counteract the other channels are usually exercises in futility.

Formal Communications

There are several pertinent reasons for the efforts of managements to convey information to employees through formal communication media such as speeches, company magazines, bulletin boards, and so on. One has already been noted: the need to insure a coordinated operation in which everyone is enabled to make the desired contribution. A second reason for formal communication is not so much a matter of informing employees as of swaying them. Sometimes management is interested in inspiring employees to make special efforts, in reinforcing their loyalty to the company by countering the claims of a union, or in explaining its own position on some matter of importance.

In some respects, the formal statement that is designed to sway rather than inform is often more of a self-reassuring ritual than a form of communication. Managements sometimes have a tendency to believe that the act of sending a message is sufficient to make it believed; or, if the message is ignored, they assume that the trouble lies merely in a lack of the necessary showmanship and editorial skill to make it convincing. For this reason, sizable sums are spent on presenting management's viewpoint to employees as attractively as possible. This effort seldom results in sizable changes of attitude on the part of the em-

ployees, and not because they are immune to a well-presented appeal
or uninterested in what management has to say or simply duped by a
better presentation of a contrary point of view. Employees are usually quite interested in what management believes. When they do not
accept the messages they are sent, it is probably because they do not
believe that the message is an accurate statement of what management really believes. And this is because they find it hard to reconcile
the statement with their own observations and preconceptions. Effective persuasion of any audience is more a matter of presenting a case
that is believable rather than a case of any artistry in communication.
For example, a company with a record of poor labor relations could
scarcely expect its intentions of turning over a new leaf to be believed, if its claims were unaccompanied by positive action. In general
it is more effective to use statements as emphasizers of past deeds
than as promises of things to come.

Another reason for the use of formal communications channels
and perhaps the most important—from the human relations standpoint, certainly the most valid—is the existence among most employee
groups of what has been referred to as "information hunger".

Survey after survey has shown that employees have an active desire to know more about their companies. This attitude is based primarily on the desire to have information that helps to get the job
done. However, information hunger also extends to matters that are
not directly related to the job, such as policy formation and internal
politics. The motivation for this hunger is seldom a matter of altruism
or idle curiosity; it expresses the need of working people to know
whether, and if so how, changes in the organization's internal environment may affect them.

This hunger is not so much for the information itself as for easy
access to it. Stanley Peterfreund, a management consultant, has given
the following description of this phenomenon, based on studies of the
internal communications systems of several large companies:

Employees often care more about being able to get information when they
need it than about actually having the specific details in hand. The following comments are typical:

"Mine is the only department to be in. Everyone says so. It's the way
you're treated. You're given freedom to express yourself, and you're heard.
It makes you want to listen more when others are talking. I guess it's just
the whole atmosphere in which we work."

"It's not so much that I have anything to say; more that, if I did, somebody would listen. It's knowing that you can tell somebody something, and you can get such-and-such information when and if you need it." (8)

Access to information, or to a hearing for one's ideas, is a dignifying and reassuring experience. It demonstrates a respect for the individual's ability to use information constructively, as well as for his ability to draw conclusions from the absence of information. Whether the individual actually needs the information to do his job is irrelevant. What *is* relevant is that his *total* working environment is intelligible, and that his ability to understand that environment is respected.

Consequently it is a prime function of management to provide access for the employee to any information that is not confidential and in which the employee expresses an interest. This is difficult to do in a systematic way. Any attempt to present information about a company in too encyclopedic a fashion runs the risk of inundating the employees in what are, to them, irrelevancies. On the other hand, it would be impossible to anticipate precisely those subjects about which each employee might be wondering about at any given moment.

One unique method for providing access to information as it is required is the so-called "What's on your mind?" or "Speak-up!" program. This type of program takes various forms, but it is essentially a system whereby employees can anonymously submit questions about the company. The inquiries are routed to the person in the company who is best qualified to answer it. He then prepares a written reply, which may then be published or posted if it is of general interest or returned to the employee through a series of intermediaries, thereby effectively concealing his identity.

These systems have the advantage of providing precisely the information that is desired for the people who desire it. They also provide a rough index of what topics are of current interest to employees. However, they are hardly a panacea for information hunger. For one thing, the percentage of employees who choose to use them is usually rather low. The typical Speak-up program oftens tends to act as a grievance channel as well as a source for information. For this reason we will cover such programs more thoroughly in Chapter Six. For the moment, suffice it to say that only part of the input to these programs consist of requests for information.

Information hunger exists due to the tendency for people who already have information to assume that other people also have it. This is especially likely to happen in large organizations where managers, despite the fact that they are the natural communications link between their subordinates and the rest of the organization, often become too preoccupied with their operational duties to provide their men with the information they want or need. This can have serious repercussions on morale. As Peterfreund notes in his article:

. . . because today's large companies are usually so highly organized with public relations and personnel staffs, and usually have so many formal media of communications, many line people feel they don't have to worry about keeping their people informed, "because it's the staff's job to get the word out. . . ."

The supervisor's "use" of communications also can affect employee morale, and in turn have impact on day-to-day functions. By merely taking time to inform an employee, a supervisor can create a feeling of recognition that has a salutary effect on his work. "They care enough to tell us" is a symptom of satisfaction all too seldom found in any company. Frequently, we receive comments such as these:

"They take it for granted that since you have been in the job so long you don't need *any* information."

"You do a job your own way because no one told you differently. They come around after it's all over and ask why you did this or that."

"The boss never consults us on anything. They go right ahead by themselves—order new equipment, do something they know nothing about. Then, when it gets to us, the problems begin." (8)

Before leaving the topic of formal communications, it is very important to note that in order to be effective they must always flow simultaneously in *two* directions. That is, it would do little good to transmit information downward that employees would be unlikely to believe or unlikely to be interested in. Even if the message were plausible and pertinent, it would be necessary to determine if a message got through without distortion. For these reasons, it is necessary to open a channel of upward communication that provides feedback on employee attitudes and perceptions.

The value of upward communications does not end with effective feedback potential. Effective communication can only occur in a receptive atmosphere: that is, when the receivers are willing to give the senders a fair hearing. The attitude of the receivers—be it open or closed-minded, friendly or hostile—has a far greater effect on the ultimate fate of a message than the way in which it is sent. A receptive atmosphere cannot be created overnight. It certainly cannot be cre-

ated by formal communications alone. It is, instead, the product of the entire human relations climate of an organization. It has many determinants, among which and perhaps the most important, is the employee's perception of management's reciprocity in giving them a hearing and in attempting to understand their problems.

Effective communication—that is, communication in which the message is actually received, understood, and acted upon positively—is necessarily a dialogue. Very few adults are willing to think of themselves as passive and empty reservoirs into which other people simply pour ideas; they prefer to think that they have ideas of their own. Regardless of whether those ideas are good or bad, they want them to be heard. If no mechanism exists for assuring that their ideas are heard, they have recourse to a simple and effective revenge. They close their minds to other people's ideas. This poses an enormous problem for any large organization and a nearly insurmountable one for an organization which treats communication as largely a matter of pumping top management's views downward. It is difficult to open a dialogue where there had previously been only a monologue. Given the pyramidal power structure of most organizations and the preoccupation of most top managements with operating results, it is even difficult to maintain an established dialogue in good working order. Yet a genuine, continuing dialogue between management and employees is indispensible for effective communications.

There are various formal mechanisms for effecting upward communication. Some of these methods will be discussed in the chapters on grievance channels, appraisal and counselling, and morale. However, what might be called an "implicit mechanism" is likely to be far more effective than any formal one. This is simply the demonstrated willingness of managers at any level to listen to, or even to actively seek out, the opinions of their subordinates.

Informal Communications

The informal communications of a company consist of all of the attempts by its members to interpret their internal environment. They usually take the form of rumors, gossip, and casual exchanges of opinion that come to be regarded as fact.

Rumors result from information hunger. This does not imply that employees who are given all of the facts that are pertinent to their jobs will not concoct, spread, and believe rumors. Information hunger exists as much when people are not provided with reassuring or welcome information as when they are not provided with pertinent infor-

mation. Neither does it imply that rumors are in themselves unhealthy or competitive with the interests of the company. Rumors are seldom anything more sinister than an attempt to make the organization intelligible and to reconcile what the employees actually experience on the job with what they hope and fear. Very often a rumor begins with a plausible speculation, but its real roots lie in why it is plausible and why there is speculation at all. A rumor which has the ring of truth, and is therefore likely to be repeated and believed, must be congruent with what is already believed. If the facts are too indistinct to permit firm beliefs, a plausible rumor will be one that expresses the predominant emotion of the group, be it hope, fear, and so on. Plausibility is therefore largely a matter of linking present experience with past learning or past prejudices. To put it more directly, a rumor is an expression of what people *want* to believe and is therefore a useful diagnostic tool for indicating the underlying needs of the people who choose to believe them.

Speculation is a product of uncertainty and interest. It is useful to remember that people may feel uncertain even when they know all of the facts. Again, it is the congruence of knowledge with emotions that makes for certainty, and the inability of facts to satisfy a thirst for security, prestige, revenge, or some other emotional need that makes for uncertainty. When a strong need exists, the tendency to hope against hope that somehow it might be satisfied can render the facts unconvincing. Therefore, a group of employees who are uncertain in their own minds about how to interpret their company environment may be uninformed, dissatisfied, or both. As for interest, it goes without saying that matters of trivial importance are unlikely to arouse more than idle curiosity. The type of speculation that leads to rumors is almost always concerned with a matter of vital concern to the people involved. When interest is not keen, the rumors usually deal with a topic that represents a source of anxiety in a rather indirect way. The reason why rumors can spread so quickly and persist for so long is because the very conditions that make it likely that plausible speculations will occur also create a strong receptivity for them. The analogy of a forest fire is apt: it spreads for the same reason that it begins. Under-informed, uncertain, or insecure people *must* circulate rumors in order to make their environment more tolerable. They spread rumors not to be perverse but to be more comfortable.

The proverbial speed of the grapevine is a testimonial to how quickly people can distribute information when it fulfills a strong per-

sonal need. People in the act of spreading rumors are likely to be highly motivated—motivated, that is, to believe that their environment has become more understandable but not necessarily to believe what they are told. If you add to this speed and motivation the element of frequent repetition, you have all of the elements needed for entrenching a rumor in an almost irrefutable position. The speculations on which rumors are built are usually triggered by a significant event that is either not explained at all or not explained satisfactorily. The lack of an explanation is usually due to the fact that management believed that the event would be of little concern to the employees or that they would be unaware of it. However, the very fact that there is not satisfactory explanation may suggest to the employees that management is attempting to conceal something unpleasant. Rumors are therefore likely to portray a situation as considerably more serious than it actually is. For example, it is not uncommon for budget-conscious companies to call a temporary halt to certain activities in order to prevent costs from rising beyond projected levels. These pauses are seldom announced and indeed are often considered highly confidential. However, if the stoppage affects an activity that the employees regard as significant—such as hiring, promotions, or salary increases—it is nearly impossible to conceal the change from them, simply because they are constantly attentive to the activity as it normally occurs and can easily detect a change.

A change of this kind, once suspected or recognized, is as much a form of communication as any formal statement. It is information that affects action on the job and is transmitted quickly through the informal channel of rumor. In an attempt to reconcile the two relevant facts—that a change has occurred, but that it has not been announced or explained—the employees are quite likely to conclude that they portend something ominous. Otherwise why the suddenness and why the secrecy? Even long after the suspended program is resumed, the rumors the change generated are likely to persist. This is because the anxieties they generated usually persist. Explanations given after management recognizes this anxiety are unlikely to be very convincing, simply because it is delayed and therefore suspect of being designed to mollify rather than to inform.

A better strategy is to explain such moves in advance. Since it is difficult to anticipate *every* action that might provoke anxiety, a still better strategy would be to teach the employees something of the philosophy underlying changes that are occasionally necessary but do not necessarily imply any permanent changes of policy.

This brings us to the heart of the communications problem in most organizations. We have suggested that most employees have an interest in knowing some of the central facts and concepts that guide the over-all management of the firm. They are concerned with the sort of higher level issues about which they are often considered to be disinterested in or incapable of understanding. Yet the persistent, morale-sapping rumors that plague many organizations are usually little more than the employee's best guesses of how management perceives those very issues. Certainly no detailed or highly technical explanations are called for; periodic briefings to all employees on how management regards its major problems, and what it plans to do about them, could help to prevent needless fears and misinterpretations.

We have also suggested that management's actions—even its in-actions—are as much a form of communication as any formal statement. People read meaning into actions and are more convinced by actions than by words. To make statements that do not offer a satisfactory explanation of actions taken—or worse still, that ignore such actions—is to place the formal communications system in hopelessly unequal competition with the informal communications system.

Implicit Communications

The implicit communication channel in an organization is the least explicit of the three and therefore the hardest to refute. In essence it is not so much a medium for distributing information as an *attitude toward* information. We have already described the importance of the believability of a formal or informal message. Now we will consider the more fundamental question of how the background against which formal and informal messages are judged is itself formed.

The implicit channel includes both "information," that which is generally accepted without necessarily having a strong foundation in fact, and "noninformation," which is in the form of areas of ignorance that persist because they are traditionally unquestioned. These are obviously highly intangible considerations. Yet, as we examine each it should become clear that these less familiar byways of the total communications system within an organization can have a decidedly tangible effect upon its operations.

One form of implicit communication is what has been referred to as the company "image." This is a rather loose, hard-to-define concept that refers to those qualities that people tend to associate with a given company. It is as if certain human characteristics were somehow perceived in an organization as a whole, thus giving rise to ex-

pectations that the organization could be expected to behave in certain predictable ways. The image of a company is therefore a sort of collective mythology about it, to which many people subscribe without ever defining it very clearly or testing its validity.

Images have a number of important qualities that, despite their intangible nature, cannot be ignored. The first is that images can have very tangible effects upon a company's relationships with its "public." The quality of job applicants, the response of sales prospects, and to some extent even the attitude of courts and legislators may be affected by the generalities that people are willing to accept as truth about a company they know only by reputation. Second, images are more likely to be started by something dramatic or bizarre than by a balanced assessment of the facts. People who are not brought into frequent confrontation with the facts have an unfortunate, but altogether human, tendency to believe whatever fits their preconceived ideas or stirs their imagination. While few if any company images are altogether fictitious, most contain considerable elements of exaggeration based on dramatic but unrepresentative examples. Quite often an image is formed simply as the result of constant, unchallenged repetition of a rumor. But whereas a rumor is at least a statement that can be analyzed and tested, an image is far more insidious. It is not a statement but an impression: a set of qualities, usually tinged with emotion, that happen to be associated in the listener's mind with the rumor (or fact) that he hears. This impression in turn affects the way in which he discusses the company with others—his choice of words, his inflection, and other subtle ways of suggesting the qualities he associates with it. Third, images tend to persist long after the specific incident or rumor that triggered them has ceased to exist. This is partly because images are so vague that they are hard to define, much less refute; partly because they are usually given the greatest credence by people without much access to facts that might change their minds; and partly because there is a certain comfort to be derived from believing that institutions exist that are repositories of all good (or all bad) qualities.

To illustrate these points, perhaps it will suffice to quote a capsule description of the Ford Motor Company in the period just after World War II. This description, prepared by a reputable business journalist, is a succinct summary of what was common knowledge about the company at the time:

Henry Ford['s] . . . enormous energy, will power and inventiveness were totally harnessed to the Ford Motor Company. He ran it as a one-man show and its early success is in large measure owing to this. The automo-

bile business was new then, and one-man control of a small enterprise had lots to recommend it. But times changed. Henry did not. He still tried to run a billion-dollar company as if it were just bigger but no different than in the twenties.

Thus by 1946 Ford was going through a crisis of the first magnitude. The company's management was demoralized and for good reason. Under old Henry's one-man dictatorship, executives had been periodically demoted so they wouldn't get "uppity," the "ins" ruled over savage little empires, the "outs" were apt to learn of their severance by one day discovering their office furniture piled in the corridor. Its work force was even more demoralized. After years of repression and Harry Bennett's use of thugs as instruments of corporate labor policy, workers employed wildcat strikes and slowdowns to express their collective hatred. Individually they resorted to sabotage. A nut was left off here, a weld there, or live rats and pop bottles were walled up in Lincoln door panels. . . .

It was only when *young* Henry took matters in his own hands and got Ernest Breech in to help him that Ford became an up-to-date corporation, its organizational deficiencies remedied, its cost-control problems resolved, its management vacuum filled, and its labor troubles mitigated. (9:16.)

It took Ford years, and no little expense, to live down the reputation that incidents such as these had given it. The image of individual insecurity at all levels, and of sudden, almost arbitrary changes of management, was perhaps deserved. But it can hardly be doubted that as this image reached the wider community in which the company operated, it affected choices made by prospective employees and prospective purchasers, and may even have had a share in affecting choices made by legislators in the New Deal era. How it affected the productivity and cooperativeness of the employees is amply illustrated in the quotation.

But there is a still subtler form of implicit communication within an organization, with a much more potent impact on its operations. This has been referred to as the relative "transparency" or "opacity" of communication itself. That is, how accessible and intelligible is the information that people need not only to do their jobs but also to feel sufficiently secure and competent to do their jobs properly?

Some recent research in England (10) provides some valuable insights into this problem. Although the research was conducted in hospitals, its essential findings have been verified in industrial contexts and seem applicable to any operation whose efficiency depends upon reliable internal communication. This research was conducted by R. W. Revans, of the Manchester College of Science and Technology, and several of his students. It took place over a four-year period at some fourteen general hospitals, mainly in the north of England. The

primary purpose of these studies was to determine whether the quality of communication within these hospitals had a measurable effect on the efficiency of their operations.

The Manchester group chose to focus its interest on two major variables: (1) attrition of student nurses (several of these hospitals had nursing schools); and (2) length of patient stay. About half of the young women who enter nursing traning in England fail to complete it; for this reason alone a study which would throw some light on the reasons for this enormous wastage of talent and resources would be justified. The length of patient stay is a complex variable. It is subject on the one hand to the need to limit costs and allocate scarce hospital services and on the other hand to the need to assure that each patient receives the optimum benefit of such services. Any means by which the economic problem could be alleviated without reducing the hospitals' ability to help the patient to recovery would of course be welcome. Since they were seeking correlations between "hard," verifiable events such as resignations or patient discharges, on the one hand, and "soft" or impressionistic events, such as the willingness of a superior to be questioned by a subordinate on the other, a unique combination of methods was required. In general the research team subjected administrative records to statistical analysis, looking for differences that should not be reasonably dismissed as accidental or meaningless. To get at subjective impressions and attitudes, they used direct observations (such as, for example, actually counting the number of questions addressed during the day to a particular supervisor), as well as opinion survey questionnaires.

The Manchester group noted that some hospitals experienced a considerably higher rate in loss of student nurses than others. After ruling out several possible causes (such as leaving to be married or leaving for a better-paying job), they concluded that the difficulty was partly a matter of the *size* of the hospitals. That is, the larger ones had the highest loss rates. Since size was hardly likely to cause attrition by itself, the researchers looked for some effect of size that might, in turn, reduce the willingness or ability of the girls to remain in the program. They found it in the ability of the institution to make the student's role intelligible to her. Any training assignment requires that the student learn to handle problems in a way that their superiors will regard as proper. When the job involves judgment rather than the unquestioning repetition of routines, it is essential that the student understand not merely the right thing to do but more importantly the reason why it is right. Without this comprehension, the student

faces the next similar problem without any assurance that it can be solved. When this general insecurity, which any trainee may face, is complicated by the added responsibility for human life, the excessive insecurity among nursing students is easy to imagine. If the lack of guidance is not remedied quickly, the resulting emotional distress can lead to illness, absence, and finally to failure or resignation from the program.

A student nurse's job in a large hospital is not necessarily more difficult than the same job in a smaller hospital. What may very well be more difficult, however, is access to the information she needs to feel capable of handling her job. Since this is a subtle point, it is necessary to dwell on it for a moment. None of the hospitals studied by the Manchester group failed to *instruct* their students in the formal, pedagogical sense. Some, however, were doing a better job than others in explaining, clarifying, and responding to questions than others. In other words, they not only sent information, but they also responded to feedback indicating how well that information had been received. In those hospitals where information flowed in a continuous loop from the professional staff to the student nurses and back again, the loss rate of student nurses tended to be low. Where it flowed essentially in one direction—from staff to students—but was blocked in its return flow by the inaccessibility, disinterest, or active discouragement of questioning by the professional staff, the loss rate of student nurses tended to be high. Although blockages of this kind are perhaps more likely to occur in large organizations (due simply to difficulty of maintaining a communications loop among large numbers of people) communications problems are actually more a matter of attitudes than of size. The Manchester group found that the attitudes of the highest officials in the hospital tended to filter down through the various hierachical levels to the ward nurses and the students working under their direction. There was, in other words, a definable atmosphere throughout a hospital that either welcomed or discouraged the creation of a communications loop.

Of course the significance of all this goes well beyond nursing schools and hospitals. Any organization must convey to its members not only what they are expected to do but also the emotional reassurrance that they will be able to do it. This requires that information flow in a continuous, two-way loop. When it is understood that there are certain questions that one just doesn't ask, or certain rules or traditions that one just doesn't question, the loop is disrupted. An opportunity for learning is blocked. When people cannot learn, they can

only be guided by their preconceptions and their emotions. This may generate a gradually rising sense of inadequacy, as in the case of many of the student nurses, or a feeling of outrage and injustice, as in the case of many industrial workers who are told *what* to do but never *why*. Interestingly, the Manchester group found that employee turnover of all kinds was highest in hospitals where the communications flow was weakest. Wherever the various staff levels were reluctant to approach superiors with questions or suggestions, wherever the feeling was widespread that those in charge knew what was best and those beneath them had to do as they were told, turnover rates for all types of personnel tended to be high.

One really intriguing finding of the Manchester group is that patients apparently recover faster in hospitals with an effective internal communications loop than in those without one. The average length of patient stay for various selected diagnostic categories is shorter where communications are more effective. Since it proved impossible to attribute this phenomenon to external factors (such as differing treatment philosophies among physicians), the Manchester group concluded that it probably had something to do with communication. The validity of this conclusion will have to be tested by further research. This same observation also applies to the Manchester group's speculation that the patient's recovery is aided by an emotional certainty that he will recover and that he is in good hands, and that this certainty is more likely to be given by a staff that will answer his questions and calm his fears than by one that simply insists that he follow its instructions.

Grievance Channels

One of the main advantages of having available an effective communications loop is that it provides a correcting mechanism for inequities and injustices. Employees who know that any complaints they may have will be heard and dealt with fairly need not fear that they will be victimized by either the system or their supervisor. Those who have no such assurance of being heard are never secure from the threat of unfair treatment, even if it never occurs.

A grievance channel is any mechanism for calling attention to an instance in which the ordinary rules of work create an unjustifiable hardship or in which a first-line management decision appears to be unfair. The extreme importance of such channels is underscored by the fact that formal grievance-handling machinery is at the core of most union contracts, and that many unorganized companies have deemed it wise to establish grievance procedures of their own.

A grievance is essentially a challenge to a particular application of management power. It therefore tends to be viewed by both managers and employees in terms of their own attitudes toward power. One often finds rather embittered attitudes on both sides. Thus

among traditionally minded (theory X) managers, grievances are sometimes regarded as insubordination or as attempts to usurp management's authority by entangling it in endless petty controversy. Among the more proletarian-minded employees, it is often assumed that any protests are automatically unwelcome and that anyone rash enough to express his dissatisfaction openly is only marking himself for future managerial revenge.

The widespread existence of extreme attitudes of both types resulted in the establishment of formal grievance-handling machinery. The function of these programs is to permit the employee to seek relief from his complaints without having to fear that the act of complaining will be penalized. When the machinery is established by negotiation (as in the case of union contracts), management's rights are also protected by a detailed delineation of what kinds of problems are and are not covered by the agreement. The inevitable unclear cases are usually handled by some form of arbitration or mediation. Formal grievance machinery usually provides some sort of an advocate to represent the employee's case. Frequently the shop steward has this responsibility. This is based partly on the theory that many workers are too timid or too inarticulate to present their cases effectively, and partly because the shop steward represents the entire might of the union. In large unionized companies, the processing of grievances can be a rather legalistic procedure requiring a great deal of attention. It also requires shop stewards to devote a considerable proportion of their working time to the handling of union affairs. This results in one of the perennial questions in contract bargaining sessions: How much time (at full pay) should the stewards devote to union activities—which consist principally of grievance-handling?

Underlying all this cumbersome but frequently necessary apparatus is the question of what constitutes fairness, and why it is that under certain circumstances workers tend to feel that they are not being treated fairly. It should be clear that in any discussion of human relations, it makes little sense to answer this question in a judicial or philosophic way. Rather it is a matter of perception; and perception, as we know, can be greatly distorted by emotions.

Occasionally one has to deal with what some psychiatrists call injustice collectors—people who are so soured by mistrust and envy that they encounter what looks to them like unfairness at every turn. More often, people with unwarped minds learn to expect unfairness, either because management doesn't take the trouble to explain its actions or because of a history of actual unfairness that leads to long-

standing grudges. Still more often, employees are willing to judge their companies by their actions toward them, but they retain a sensitive pride in their own individuality that does not permit them to take lightly any indication that they may be cheated or dealt with arbitrarily. Whatever its source—in morbid mistrust, management abuses, or normally tender egos—a sensitivity to questions of fairness is extremely important among working people.

Where formal grievance channels do not exist, the ingenuity of an aggrieved worker will often create one. Instances have been recorded, for example, in which employees who were angered at the attitude of their local managers placed an advertisement in a prominent newspaper announcing their availability for hire by other companies. To make certain that the point was not lost, a clipping of the advertisement "happened" to appear on the desk of a key executive on the day it was published. Less theatrical means of calling attention to grievances have also been improvised. The most common is the unsigned letter to a top executive. This tactic is sometimes ineffective, since it is inherently unfair to the managers it accuses. A more effective means of calling attention to a grievance is to bring it to the attention of someone who acts as an informal intermediary between management and employees. Executive secretaries and older employees, especially those who are on the verge of retirement, often play this role. So do personnel department employees.

No matter how people contrive to present their case, all grievance channels share this characteristic: they circumvent the first-line or the local manager. Very often they represent an attempt to reverse a first-line decision or to change a first-line attitude. In one sense, the development of grievance channels represents one of the keystones of modern industrial democracy. They guarantee that whatever rights are due to the individual by company policy or tradition will not be denied to him by supervisory fiat or negligence. Often the mere existence of effective grievance procedures is more important, in the long run, than whether they are actually used very often. It is not so much a problem of there being too many arbitrary supervisors as of protecting each individual against even just one such supervisor. This is especially true in large organizations, in which it is so easy for an employee to feel isolated from the center of authority, and therefore very much at the mercy of local management.

One mechanism that has proven to be an effective grievance channel in large organizations, and in companies that are not unionized, is the open door policy. It gets its name from the concept that

the door of every manager from the first-line manager to the president himself should always be open to any employee who wants to present a grievance. The open door policy assumes that an employee who is dissatisfied for any reason will first discuss the problem with his immediate superior. If the employee continues to feel dissatisfied, he is then supposed to present his case to the second-line manager. If this discussion does not lead to an acceptable solution he then goes to a still higher executive. Eventually, the employee may present his case to the vice president in charge of personnel or to the president himself. At each stage below that of the president, it is the duty of the manager hearing the case to investigate it fully and then decide whether, in the light of company policy, the employee's arguments are justified. If they are, the manager must revise the decision to which the employee objects; if they are not, the manager must try to demonstrate to the employee why he is in error.

In actual practice, the successful use of the open door policy depends on a high degree of managerial skill and above all on a history of enlightened labor relations. It cannot be introduced as a panacea for labor problems that have already become severe. Neither can it be implemented successfully by managers who would actually use it as a means of selling unpalatable decisions to employees. The open door policy requires a highly developed degree of mutual trust and a mutual insistence on fairness. This includes a willingness to admit that one has made a mistake, or at least a willingness to accept decisions that are equitable if not wholly satisfactory. This kind of willingness is the result of a mutual learning process that may require years to reach fruition. Therefore, an effective open door policy is more of a goal to be sought than an easily introduced expedient.

The difficulties with the open door policy begin with its first assumption. Quite often an employee will *not* wish to bring his dissatisfaction to the attention of his supervisor. He may prefer to suffer in silence, in order to take advantage of whatever rewards the supervisor will presumably distribute to uncomplaining employees. He may perhaps fear that having once complained he will thereafter be suspected of being a malcontent, so that his statements will be discounted and his abilities overlooked. At worst, the employee may feel that to complain is to draw attention to one's self and that unobtrusiveness is the best guarantee of job security. When the employee is unwilling to try to seek relief for his grievances from his immediate superior, he may bottle up his feelings or confide them to someone outside of management, either of which defeats the purpose of the open

door policy. He may instead take his case directly to a higher level manager: this approach preserves the open door system but brings disadvantages of its own. First, it may overload executives with problems of a relatively petty nature that should be settled at lower levels. Second, it places executives in the position of apparently (or even actually) undercutting the first-line manager's authority. This can result in efforts by the supervisors to suppress overt dissent, which also defeats the purpose of the open door policy. It may also lead to a type of management that endures poor employee discipline in order to avoid the "blackmail" of a direct appeal to higher management.

Once an employee has exercised his right to go over the head of his manager, it is very difficult to achieve a settlement that all parties will regard as just. If the case is decided in favor of the employee, the manager is bound to feel a certain resentment. The same would be true of the employee if the case were decided in favor of the manager. While a decision may be objectively fair, it is seldom feasible to try to persuade either party that they were in the wrong. Rather the goal is to seek a solution that is not merely fair but also tolerable to both sides. After all, the ultimate objective of any appeals procedures is not only to do justice but also to permit the parties to go on working together if at all possible. For all of these reasons, the open door policy achieves its main value from its availability rather than its use. At its best it is a wholesome discipline to which management submits and an arbiter to which employees may turn with confidence should the need ever arise. It is designed to help create the conditions that make its frequent use unnecessary.

We have already referred to the Speak-up! program in connection with its function as a communications device. This kind of program provides a way for any employee to submit a confidential written inquiry on any question regarding company policy or practices and to receive an authoritative written reply, without ever revealing his identity. Because these programs are announced (and primarily intended) as a means of disseminating information, they are usually administered by a special department, which normally does not process greivances. In spite of this fact, a sizable proportion of the letters submitted under the program do not consist of inquiries at all, but are complaints or demands for review of a first-line manager's decision. In other words, employees will utilize as a grievance channel *any* mechanism that puts them into direct touch with higher management, regardless of the primary purpose for which the mechanism was designed. This is certainly true of the Speak-up! program, and for this

reason a close liaison between the communications and personnel departments is necessary for the successful operation of the program. Ideally, both departments would report to the same executive.

When Speak-up programs are used to voice a grievance, great care must be exercised to avoid settling the case with the reply. An aggrieved employee will tend, understandably, to state his case as he sees it—in terms that strengthen his claims and imply some injustice on the part of his manager. There is, of course, always another side of the story; but in view of the strict confidentiality maintained to protect the identity of the employee, it is hardly practical to conduct an adequate investigation. The reply must therefore clarify principles without providing a statement so specific that it could be cited as proof that the manager was in the wrong. This is obviously a very delicate procedure, because a reply that is too vague will be unsatisfactory to the employee. This difficulty arises from the fact that the program is designed to dispense information rather than justice. Nevertheless, it has its attractions as a grievance channel—the guarantee of anonymity is probably the greatest—and therefore its continued use as a grievance channel is inevitable.

To educate employees as to the proper purposes of each program is only a partial solution. Whenever a grievance is submitted through an information channel, the reply should include a suggestion that the writer avail himself of the company's normal grievance procedures. Whether this suggestion will work will depend, in the last analysis, on what is surely one of the most crucial variables in any organization's human relations climate: the quality of the employee-manager relationship. All grievance channels are, after all, ways of relieving the individual from the complete control of his immediate superior. They exist as a disipline to the managers and a guarantee to the employees. Their function is as much to reassure employees that justice is available as to actually dispense justice.

To the extent that grievance channels are used, some kind of flaw may be suspected in the basic relationship of the complaining individual and his manager. Either the manager has failed to win the employee's confidence, or the employee is too distrustful to work the problem out with his manager, or both. Most problems that find their way into grievance channels are of the type that can be, and usually are, settled at the first-line level. They involve such issues as shift assignments, relief time, and minor disciplinary problems. The ability of a supervisor to win the confidence of his men for his fairness is obviously a crucial variable. He must know when and how much to

compromise, what to overlook, and what to insist on. Above all, he must know how to make himself understood without being either overbearing or patronizing. In a sense, it is precisely because it is so difficult for *any* supervisor to accomplish all this in a consistently successful way that grievance channels have to be provided.

Enormous efforts have been devoted to making first-line supervisors more capable of controlling without antagonizing. The problem is usually thought of in terms of selecting supervisors who are sensitive, who know how to handle people, or in terms of teaching supervisors to be more adroit in their relationships with their subordinates. There is little doubt that better selection and training can help, but very often the quality of employee-supervisory relations is more of a symptom of other relationships than of any failings on the part of the supervisors. Supervisors, after all, have supervisors of their own; it is entirely understandable that they are more often sensitive to the desires of their superiors than to those of their subordinates. The supervisor receives cues from his own superior as to what is expected of him, just as any employee does; the supervisory style that he develops is at least partly a reflection of his efforts to please his own boss.

The triumph of human relations (at least in a theoretical sense) has been so complete that there are very few second-line managers who do not expect the supervisors reporting to them to maintain good morale among the employees reporting to *them*. The problem is that this expectation is taken for granted and is voiced only occasionally. What the supervisor is likely to hear from management is a relatively constant emphasis on achieving production targets, staying within budgets, and winning new contracts. Reminders that people are important too are likely to be heard less frequently. It is hardly surprising, therefore, if many supervisors conclude that their own performance is being measured chiefly in terms of dollars-and-cents results, and that as long as no one is complaining too loudly, their relations with employees need not require too much attention.

A significant part of the human relations climate at the first-line level is determined by the patterns of emphasis that higher levels of management adopt in communicating with supervisors. As with all communications, actions speak louder than words. If promotions go to the supervisor whose budgetary performance is exemplary and whose subordinates are unobtrusively discontented, why worry about morale? The result is an all too common philosophy that hardly anyone worries very much about morale until it deteriorates to a point where it is no longer unobtrusive—a point at which it is usually too

late to rescue the situation anyway. When grievence channels are put to frequent use, management tends to believe that something is wrong with its first-line managers. Something usually *is* wrong, but it is often a matter of supervisors adopting the values and standards implied by management's own actions, rather than any deficiencies of their own.

It is extremely important to recognize that any organization is in reality an interlocking *system* in which every component has an influence, however subtle and indirect, on every other component. Grievances arise from confrontations between specific individuals; but they may find themselves in opposing positions as the result of forces set in motion elsewhere, rather than because of stubbornness or unreasonableness on their parts. It is true, however, that a capable manager will always try to reconcile the conflicting pressures placed upon him from above and below in a way that is if not ideal, at least satisfactory to both sides. This constant balancing of competing interests is the essence of the manager's job and its most convincing raison d'être.

In a subsequent chapter, we will consider the question of morale in greater detail. For the moment it will suffice to make three points: (1) the availability of effective grievance channels is essential for the long-term maintenance of morale; (2) it is equally important that supervisors constantly demonstrate their fairness, respect for, and interest in each of the individuals reporting to them; (3) without detracting in any way from the importance of grievance channels or the man-manager relationship, it must be recognized that other variables that are not ordinarily thought of in the context of human relations can have a profound effect on morale. Among these are organization structure, personnel selection policies, the external job market, and a company's internal growth.

The utility of effective grievance channels is perhaps most vividly illustrated in connection with the introduction of methods changes designed to improve productivity. Such changes are becoming increasingly common in industry; as the pace of automation and technological change quicken, they are likely to occur even more frequently. Nearly any change in working methods costs something in human terms. Morale may decline, loyalty and diligence may weaken, and cooperation may turn into resistance. For these reasons, management should attempt to minimize the human costs involved in any contemplated change.

A study by David Sirota of International Business Machines Cor-

poration (11) throws considerable light on the role played by grievance channels in the accomplishment of change. Sirota analyzed the
results of an extensive questionnaire that had been completed by
some 1200 factory workers, all of whom were engaged in repetitive
types of work. Prior to being given the questionnaire, about 83 percent of these workers had been placed under a work measurement
system in which their output was rated against standards set by industrial engineers. The remainder were not working under measured
standards. It is important to realize that in the plants where this study
was made, measured work standards of any kind were not traditional,
and their introduction represented quite an innovation to the employees.

The first finding of the study was hardly surprising: morale in the
unchanged (that is, nonmeasured) departments was noticeably higher than in those departments where work measurement had been introduced. The new system brought feelings that pressure on employees had been increased and that the company had become less
concerned with the well-being of the employee. Significantly, however, these feelings were by no means uniform among the employees
working against measured standards. Although the *average* morale of
the group was undoubtedly down, there was considerable variation
within the group.

In searching for factors that might distinguish the workers whose
morale had been only slightly affected by the measurement program
from those whose morale had been markedly affected, Sirota examined the adequacy of grievance channels. He defined *adequacy* by ac-
cepting the employee's evaluation of the safety of resorting to the
grievance procedure. Thus, if an employee, in responding to the questionnaire, had indicated his belief that managers would correct unfair
workloads if these were brought to their attention, or that an appeal
to higher management could be made without fear of retaliation, his
own grievance channels were considered to be adequate. If he felt
that managers would not change production expectations that the
men complained of, or that it would not be safe to appeal the case,
his grievance channels were considered to be inadequate.

When the men in the measurement program were divided according to their own rating of the adequacy of their grievance channels, some striking differences in morale appeared. The men who
rated their grievance channels as adequate were significantly more
positive than the others in their attitudes toward the company, the
amount of work expected of them, and the measurement program it-

self. Thus it appeared that while the introduction of a change of this type lowered morale, the effect could be considerably mitigated by the kind of employee-manager relationships that assure the availability and safety of grievance channels.

Of course, as with all correlational studies, it might be argued that cause and effect have been reversed: that men who felt positively toward the company would tend to assume that their grievance channels were adequate, and so on. Such arguments can never be disposed of entirely, but in this case they are at least cast in considerable doubt by another finding. Some of the groups studied reported considerably more trouble than others in reaching the new performance standards. Even where the difficulty was great, morale tended to be no worse than in groups that met the standards easily, *provided grievance channels were adequate.* On the other hand, where meeting the standards was difficult and grievance channels were poor, morale tended to be quite low.

Sirota argues that a marked decline in morale following the introduction of new methods for increasing productivity need not be fatalistically accepted as inevitable, and that it can be controlled through intelligent planning. The condition of grievance channels in use prior to the introduction of such a change should be carefully checked, and strengthened where necessary. Unfortunately, the strengthening process cannot be accomplished quickly. We have already noted that adequate grievance channels develop through a gradual process of learning. From this it follows that a company that has had the foresight to develop and preserve adequate grievance channels for its employees can probably make the transition to new work methods at considerably less human cost than one that has not fostered such a development.

Performance Appraisal and Employee Counseling

The two processes of performance appraisal and employee counseling are usually mentioned together, and they are often considered to be among the foremost tools of an enlightened human relations policy. Whether they have actually advanced the cause of human relations very far is a question that has been argued endlessly. It is quite clear, however, that in the process of trying to implement these supposedly straightforward programs, we have had to learn a great deal about how intense and complex the relations of working people to their supervisors really are.

Performance appraisal means a formal rating of how well an employee has handled his assigned duties during a given period of time. These ratings are generally considered useful for salary administration, the identification of training needs and of promotable individuals, and for determining whether an individual is sufficiently competent to be retained at his present job level. Employee counseling means a deliberate, formal effort to help the employee to become

more valuable to the company by means of personal discussions. These discussions are usually held on a regularly scheduled basis (annually or semiannually) by the employee and his immediate superior. The subjects discussed usually include a review of the employee's job performance during the previous period and a consideration of what steps ought to be taken during the coming period to improve or strengthen his performance. As a rule, counseling is based on the appraisal; that is, the major function of the counseling interview is to advise the employee of the results of the manager's appraisal of his performance. This practice is based on the assumption that the employee's knowledge of where he stands in the manager's eyes is likely to improve his performance.

We have already mentioned that an effective appraisal and counseling program is extremely difficult to administer. A major reason for this failure is that the results of such programs often fall considerably short of their objectives. A large number of proposals have been advanced for modifying these programs so as to make them more effective. Not the least of these proposals is that the combination of appraisal and counseling be done away with altogether, on the grounds that it is inherently unworkable in the hands of a vast majority of managers.

Appraisal and counseling can properly be regarded as an experiment. If it is to work well at all, it will clearly require a level of sophistication we are still struggling to attain. But there is very little reason to write the experiment off as a total loss, if only because it has not yet had the chance it deserves to be studied and improved. The objectives for which it is designed are certainly important enough to justify a continued effort to adjust the methods used in appraisal and counseling to the inconvenient realities they have helped us to discover.

This chapter will first of all examine the reasons that have been given for having a formal appraisal and counseling program. It will then review the major criticisms that have been leveled against these programs and the rebuttals to the criticisms. Next it will analyze some of the psychological ambiguities that seem to be involved in the process including: what knowing "where you stand" actually means, the effect of expectations on interview results, the problem of a manager having to "play God," and of the conflicting goals of the process. We shall also consider the counseling interview itself, and how both the manager and the employee might learn to make better use of it.

Reasons for and Against Appraisal and Counseling

The most commonly given reason for appraisal and counseling programs is that the employee should know where he stands with management. It is held that in a democratic industrial order the employee has a *right* to know how his work and his future prospects are evaluated. The very concept that secret dossiers might exist that determine a man's future and reflect on his past is inherently repugnant to most people. It is also held that most employees *want* to know where they stand. This assertion has been borne out by innumerable opinion surveys showing a lack of certainty on this issue and a desire for clearer feedback from management. Lastly, it is held that an employee who is told where he stands is more likely to improve his productivity than one who does not, if only because he knows where to concentrate his efforts more effectively.

This last point deserves some elaboration, since it is the most persuasive reason for telling employees where they stand. One of the cardinal tenets of the scientific management school is that a man's effectiveness on the job is significantly affected by his understanding of what is expected of him. If management's expectations are made clear to him, he can handle his job exactly as its designers intended that he should. The appraisal interview would then function as a sort of periodic correction of any errant tendencies that may have developed in the interim. The trouble with this formulation is that it is altogether too neat and simple. On many jobs, what management wants may be difficult to express and still more difficult for the employee to achieve. Showing more imagination or more alertness are examples of what is frequently desired of an employee. Further, even when an employee understands what is expected of him, this knowledge will not necessarily motivate him to achieve it. Most employees have expectations of their own toward management, which require a hearing and some kind of feedback if the employees are to be at all receptive to what management has to say.

Despite these difficulties, a number of arguments can be advanced in favor of appraisal and counseling. Their total weight builds a powerful case for continuing to use the process. For example, it is said that an effective appraisal and counseling program can build and sustain morale by demonstrating the company's fairness and its interest in the future of each employee. That is, entirely apart from the immediate effects of the program, its very existence can serve as the

symbol of an attitude that employees would find reassuring. (Communication by symbol, while seldom deliberate, is a potent way of making a point.) The indirect result of management's having made a gesture of this kind might be an enhancement of employee loyalty and productivity.

It has also been suggested that an appraisal and counseling program is an effective management development tool in at least three ways. The most obvious of these is in the identification of potential managers and grooming of them by means of advice and encouragement. The second is the acquisition, by the individual manager, of a more realistic understanding of the employee's point of view. This in turn would presumably lead to better communications and more effective leadership. The third aspect is certainly the subtlest and perhaps the most important of all: the tendency of an appraisal and counseling program to *compel* managers to be more attentive to the performance and needs of their subordinates. Without such continuing attention, the counseling interview itself becomes an obvious fiasco that reveals the manager's own deficiencies with an all too embarrassing clarity. Indeed it has been said only half-facetiously that if all managers were as responsive to employees as they should be, a formal appraisal and counseling program would be unnecessary; since they are not, such a program forces them to become more responsive than they otherwise might be.

It has also been argued that appraisal and counseling helps to develop the competence of employees more quickly and more fully. This is accomplished by permitting them to correct errors and bad habits before they become ingrained and to concentrate on the most critical aspects of their work. This argument assumes, of course, that such corrections would not normally be provided by supervisors, at least not emphatically enough to be effective. Unhappily, this assumption is all too likely to be warranted in many cases.

Finally, it is held that appraisal and counseling programs are necessary for dealing fairly and effectively with inadequate performers. Such people deserve both a reasonable opportunity to correct their deficiencies and whatever assistance management can give them. If a satisfactory level of performance can be achieved, the company will have preserved both its own financial investment in the individual and his more precious investment (to him) of time in the company. If the effort fails, it will at least not have occurred through neglect, and a discreet and decent departure can be arranged.

Against these claims for appraisal and counseling, a number of

serious charges have been leveled. These include the resistance of managers to the program, varying degrees of employee satisfaction with the results, a frank skepticism as to whether many employees really do want to know where they stand, and the difficulty of demonstrating whether the program achieves worthwhile results.

Management resistance to the program shows up in various ways. Probably the most common is simply not to hold the interviews at all, on the grounds that the employees already know where they stand because they constantly are given (by management) feedback on their performance. Another frequent excuse is that the demands on the manager's time are so great that there is no time left for appraisal and counseling after he attends to more urgent matters. Still another form of resistance is to conduct interviews that are so vague or cautiously phrased that the employee learns very little that might be useful.

Social research has repeatedly shown that managers tend to overrate the degree to which their subordinates feel confident of knowing where they stand. Informal feedback from one's manager, although it is undoubtedly a requisite of effective management, is seldom as frequent or as emphatic as it would have to be to eliminate the employee's uncertainty that he *really* knows how his work has been appraised. As for the argument that there is not enough time available to prepare and hold counseling interviews, this is just another way of saying that the manager does not consider the process important enough to make time available for it.

Why do some managers tend to resist the implementation of appraisal and counseling programs, especially when very few of them would quarrel with the objectives of the program? Douglas McGregor (whom we encountered earlier in connection with theories X and Y) argued that this resistance, far from being reprehensible, is actually a form of "unconscious wisdom" by means of which the manager steers clear of what would otherwise be a harmful situation for both himself and his subordinates. (12) To have to justify one's judgments of another man to that man is, according to this view, an inherently impossible process because it puts both men's egos and both men's qualifications for their jobs on trial simultaneously. If attempted too frankly, the process bruises at least one ego and makes it that much harder for the two men to work productively in the future. If attempted too cautiously, the process raises more questions than it answers and creates at least the suspicion that management has been less than candid. It is far wiser, according to McGregor, to finesse the

problem altogether by avoiding any kind of judgment of the *man* and concentrating instead on a review of how closely his accomplishments at work have approached targets that had been previously and mutually set.

The case for conventional appraisal and counseling has been stated (partially in rebuttal to McGregor) by Harold Mayfield of Owens-Illinois Glass Company (13). The essence of his argument is that while the pitfalls outlined by McGregor and other critics would be serious if they occurred very often, in actual practice they do not. According to Mayfield, managerial resistance to appraisal and counseling arises from two principal causes, both of which can be corrected: (1) a fear of getting into a situation with which they cannot cope, (2) a lack of a sense of urgency. In each case, adequate training and follow-up could relieve the problem. But not without a certain degree of insistence:

. . . a program such as the progress interview, which does not promise unalloyed pleasure or a dramatic payoff, needs a certain amount of system and pressure if it is to be applied generally in a company. . . . I have come to realize, reluctantly, that interviews of this kind will not be held by most supervisors unless they are built into the schedule as a part of standard operations. (13)

When employees who have been on the receiving end of appraisal interviews are asked their opinions of them, their replies are by no means unanimous. In general, satisfaction seems to be highest with relatively new employees, who regard the process as a sign of management's interest in helping them to progress. Satisfaction tends to be rather low with long-time employees who have not been promoted; they tend to regard the process as a futile and perhaps humiliating formality. Employees whose jobs have built-in feedback mechanisms, such as salesmen, are often less enthused about formal appraisals than those whose work must be judged impressionistically, such as administrative workers. However, these trends are inferred from large groups and therefore do not show the effects of particularly expert use of the appraisal and counseling interview. That is, in any group of managers some will be proficient at this (or any other) technique, and some will be, to put it charitably, inexpert. The effects of each cancel out the other in a large group of statistics. The net result is that we are not certain what would happen to employee satisfaction if steps were taken to increase the proficiency and willingness of managers in appraisal and counseling.

The finding that at least some employees are not at all enthused

about being appraised and counseled has called into question the basic premise of the entire process: people want to know where they stand. Apparently this is not true of the indifferent, the disillusioned, or those who know all too well that where they stand in management's esteem is not very high. It also seems that those who have been exposed to several interviews of the evasive, noncommital type are likely to lose their patience with the process. An effective appraisal and counseling program may be a preventive for widespread frustration and disillusionment, but it is hardly a panacea for those who are already frustrated and disillusioned. Indeed, in its orthodox form (that is, with emphasis upon management's evaluation of the strengths and weaknesses of the individual and his work), it may very well make things worse for them.

Very little direct evidence can be offered to the hardheaded businessman who demands clearcut evidence that the appraisal and counseling process works. This is partly because there is seldom much thought given to precisely what the program is supposed to accomplish. Appraisal and counseling are usually installed because they seem enlightened and likely to effect a general improvement of employee relations. It is therefore difficult to find some aspect of those relations that, when related to appraisal and counseling, would measure whether the process works.

The evidence both for and against appraisal and counseling is at best indirect, at least as far as its practical results are concerned. Any human performance is compounded of many factors, of which appraisal and counseling is only one. The process itself is conducted against a background of many factors that affect it, not the least of which is variation in the skill, understanding and commitment of the managers who implement it. A variety of studies could be cited that imply that under the right conditions, having such a program probably *would* make a difference—a favorable one—in a company's operations. Nevertheless, the skeptic is left with plenty of leeway for remaining unconvinced, and those who believe in appraisal and counseling programs must still do so largely on faith and on common sense.

Psychological Ambiguities

One of the reasons why it is so hard to tell a man where he stands is that *where he stands* is an ambiguous phrase. It is an American idiom rather than a precisely defined term. It refers, vaguely, to one's position relative to other people's or to a standard against which

one is being measured. It also refers to someone else's personal opinion of one's position, usually to the opinion of one's superiors. Beyond that, "to know where you stand" can mean almost anything.

The term is badly in need of a semantic analysis. To some people it seems to translate to, "When will I receive my next raise, and how much will it be?" To others it has quite another connotation, "Am I in any danger of being fired?" To still others it means, "Does anybody in this company know or care that I am here, and that I have ambitions to get ahead?" It can also mean, "What are my chances of being promoted relative to those of other men with whom I am competing?"

For some people it connotes, "Are my long years of loyal service appreciated, or am I simply taken for granted?" Yet another meaning is, "Has my work met my manager's standards or exceeded them or fallen short of them?" Sometimes it can even mean, "Does my superior like me or dislike me?" Given all this ambiguity, much of the professed failure to know where one stands can be explained easily. It is simply due to the manager's inability to anticipate exactly what an employee really wants to know. The problem is immeasurably complicated by the fact that very often the employee doesn't consciously know either. He knows well enough whether he *feels* that he knows where he stands; but the very ambiguity of the term often prevents him from knowing what kind of information would give him that feeling. Perhaps the answer to such a problem does not lie in refining the controls that assure that people are *told* where they stand, but in deciding exactly what it is we are trying to accomplish in the first place.

From a practical standpoint, being concerned about where one stands is usually a self-created or "pseudo-problem." Management's appraisals of the performance and potentialities of its employees are usually distributed in something like a normal ("bell-shaped") curve or else a curve strongly shifted toward the Good rating. This means that most people stand most of the time in a perfectly satisfactory relationship to the company as far as management is concerned, and only a minority have anything to worry about. Knowing where you stand becomes a problem only to those with whom management is not satisfied or to those whose own estimate of their worth is considerably at variance with management's. But if the where-you-stand issue is a pseudo-problem for most people, how can we explain its persistence? It cannot be analyzed away any more than it can be appraised and counseled away. After the ambiguity of the term and the superfluousness of the information are fully revealed, people *still* want to "know." Why?

The answer has a great deal to do with the real or implied power

that managers wield over employees. As the individual who is presumably better acquainted with the employee's work and abilities than anyone else, the first-line manager is in a position to become the architect of the employee's reputation. His recommendations, his written notations in a personnel file, his casual comments to other managers may all have a bearing on the employee's future. Especially where merit systems are in effect, or where there are no union guarantees of advancement and employment security, the potential effect of the supervisor on the employee's future may loom very large indeed. The supervisor's opinion of an employee, whether it is recorded in a dossier or formulated vaguely in his mind, is an instrument through which the organization can exert its power over him. It is therefore in the employee's interests to try to be sure that this form of power is exercised fairly and responsibly. He needs some influence on it, some assurance that his future is in good hands.

Even though a statement of his supervisor's opinion is not necessarily candid or complete, it provides useful feedback. If what the supervisor says is consistent with his everyday behavior toward the employee throughout the year, the employee has at least that much assurance that he knows what is shaping his future. Even the circumspection that prevents some supervisors from being entirely candid with their subordinates is in itself a form of restraint over unsupportable statements about the employee to other managers.

One does not necessarily find out where he stands by being told. The desire to know this standing is not so much a desire for information as for power; not knowing where one stands is not so much a complaint that the manager had divulged too little as much as it is that he has not demonstrated that he will exercise his power responsibly. In the last analysis, wanting to know where you stand is not motivated by vanity or curiosity but by the need for some measure of control over one's future.

Another paradox that one encounters in appraisal and counseling concerns the differing expectations of managers and employees. The conscientious manager who prepares for the annual interview carefully will usually expect the employee to emerge from it with a renewed determination to excel; while the employee who has been waiting for the interview for months will usually expect that something of dramatic importance will be revealed to him. Both are likely to be disappointed, and this in turn may make them dissatisfied with each other and with the appraisal and counseling process itself.

These situations are almost inevitable when the annual interview

is made to bear the full burden of communication that should normally have been taking place throughout the year. Regrettably, it is all too easy for two people as dependent upon each other as a supervisor and his subordinate to take each other for granted, or to leave unsaid all those things which might have made them each aware of the other's thinking. When communication is too brief, infrequent, or noncommittal, it is easy to assume that the one party has nothing to say and must therefore be interested chiefly in hearing what the other party has to say.

The fate of any particular appraisal interview is sealed long before it occurs. It has less to do with the technique of conducting an interview than with the quality of the manager-employee relationship and with their habitual ways of communicating with each other. Two men who have been reasonably candid with each other all along can regard a session, whose purpose is candor, as an opportunity to review and summarize what they both know. Two men who have gone through the motions of communicating while keeping their real opinions to themselves can only regard such a session with reluctance and suspicion. Whatever they say may stand in such sharp contrast to what they know that the interview is reduced to an exercise in compulsory insincerity.

A good appraisal interview is one in which there are no surprises, because all of the key questions will have been answered already in the course of normal daily contacts. An interview that begins with an unanswered important question cannot be fully satisfactory even if the question is answered during the interview; it *should* have been answered previously. The appraisal interview can be no stronger than the relationship that precedes it. Appraisal and counseling, like so many other human relations programs, must not be thought of as a cure for personnel problems. Instead, it is an exercise that can function effectively only within the boundaries of a fairly healthy personnel environment.

Sometimes the process suffers from an excess of managerial humility. Recognizing the profound and lasting effects that their recorded opinions might have on the careers of their subordinates, some managers are reluctant to exert their complete control by giving ratings that might be damaging to the individual's chances. This affects both the appraisals themselves and the likelihood that the employee will be able to benefit from it. It also causes the distribution of performance ratings to become rather narrow. Extreme ratings (either positive or negative) are rarely given. This makes it difficult for the

company to differentiate both its exceptionally competent employees and its borderline incompetents from the mass of ordinary employees, thereby defeating one of the major purposes of the program. In some companies an interesting semantic illusion is created by the practice of rating most employees' performance as *above average*. In effect, an *average* rating becomes a way of expressing inadequate performance without incurring the requirement (usually associated with *below average* ratings) of doing something about it. "Damning with faint praise" may get the manager's real feelings about the employee across to other managers, but it often leaves the employee unaware that he has been found wanting. The effect of this kind of managerial evasiveness can be quite serious. If his appraisal includes no clear-cut indications of faults serious enough to demand attention, the employee may simply continue to lose ground in his manager's eyes without having a fair chance to redeem himself. If he is transferred to another department on the basis of a less-than-frank proposal, he may find himself in a situation requiring performance beyond his capacities through no fault of his own. Worse still, the practice of transferring problems may make managers unwilling to rely on each other's appraisals as a basis for effecting such movements. This has the effect of freezing people in their present jobs and filling open positions with newly hired people rather than from within.

It is clear that a reluctance on the part of the manager to be completely frank in his appraisal can produce a host of evils. This reticence, however, is at least to some extent the result of the system itself. That is, in creating a program for simultaneously appraising performance and counseling employees about the results of that appraisal, we may be asking managers to reach two incompatible goals. It is quite possible that the evasiveness characterized by an unwillingness to give a true opinion is not so much a shirking of managerial duty as a recognition that the appraisal and counseling program itself is freighted with too much responsibility.

We noted at the beginning of this chapter that the two processes of appraisal and counseling are usually considered together, as if they were integrally related. This traditional assumption stems in part from the idea that workers will become more efficient if they know where they stand. Our analysis stated that while they may not always become more efficient, employees will usually feel more secure if the results of the appraisal process are disclosed to them. Finally, we noted that the presumably straightforward process of telling people about the quality of their performance frequently breaks down because the process becomes a thicket of ambiguities and delicate psy-

chological confrontations. Basically, appraisal serves the needs of the organization. It is a necessary inventory of human resources. To the extent that appraisal serves the individual at all, it does so indirectly and uncertainly. Basically, counseling serves the employee. It provides him with both guidance on where to concentrate his efforts and the indispensable emotional support of knowing that someone in authority is thinking about his (the employee's) future. To the extent that counseling serves the company, it does so secondarily and uncertainly. Why then should the two processes be linked? They cannot be entirely separated, of course, but it is neither necessary nor desirable that they be based upon each other. Appraisal can and should be uninhibited by the necessity of confrontations between the evaluator and the evaluated. Counseling can and should be based as much on the employee's aspirations, suggestions, likes and dislikes as on the manager's opinions about the employee's work.

As a practical matter, appraisal results are of interest to management only in those extreme (and therefore rare) cases where the appraisal requires some sort of action. When a man is qualified for a promotion or a salary increase, or when his work is not up to standard, management needs to know about it. But these situations should be acted on *when they occur*, which means that for all practical purposes the report and the action will take place outside the context of the formal appraisal system. For that vast majority of employees who do not require such attention at any given time, an elaborate appraisal is irrelevant as far as the company's needs are concerned. It is also a potential source of misunderstanding and needless resentment as far as the employee is concerned. For such people, it should be possible to cover the appraisal aspect of their counseling session on an exception basis. That is, if something about their work is sufficiently out of line to require being brought to their attention, they should be told about it when it becomes necessary. If there are no such matters to be discussed, the question of appraisal can be dealt with simply by noting that the employee's work has been entirely satisfactory; the interview can then proceed to really important matters.

The Counseling Interview

Undoubtedly the most important purpose of the counseling interview is to help the employee to improve or extend his competence. He must, in other words, be encouraged to *learn*—about his job, the technology that supports and may change his job, about his company,

and about the internal and external environments in which it operates. Very little of that learning can reasonably be expected to occur *during* the interview. If learning occurs at all, it will be afterward.

If we analyze the counseling interview in terms of the role it might play in such a learning process, it becomes clear that the employee himself must carry a heavier share of the responsibility for the interview than has traditionally been the case. Indeed, the traditional role assigned to the employee, that of a passive audience who is expected to absorb and accept everything that his manager tells him, could scarcely be less conducive to learning. The kind of personal growth process that the counseling interview can encourage is the result of an active inquiry by the learner. The manager's role in such a process is not to teach, much less to convince the employee of the rightness of particular viewpoint; it is to respond as realistically as possible to the employee's inquiry and to guide and encourage his efforts to grow. Viewed in this light, some of the more agonizing problems of the traditional counseling interview becomes superfluous. For example, the manager's preparation of his case, his search for incidents to hold in reserve in case a statement is challenged, his rehearsal of ways to keep control of the interview to prevent it from becoming a spontaneous discussion, can all be dispensed with. The manager is no longer required to pass judgment or to justify his opinions. Instead, he is required to discover what the employee thinks about his present job and his future prospects and to respond as helpfully as he can to what he learns.

The employee shoulders the responsibility for his own develop ment. He is the one who must do most of the preparation for the interview. He must review his accomplishments in the light of his aspirations, decide what changes to seek and what complaints to make, and determine what goals to set for himself and what avenues to follow toward those goals. In effect, he is asked to assess for himself where he stands in the light of his own desires. The very act of preparing for such a conference, and the very knowledge that such conferences will occur periodically is in itself a device that motivates the employee *to examine his situation and the reasons for his satisfaction or dissatisfaction with it.* This kind of examination, if conducted seriously enough and regularly enough, is a basis on which real growth can occur.

However, it would be fatuous to assume that all of the problems associated with appraisal and counseling would disappear simply by

separating the processes and putting the main responsibility for the counseling interview on the employee. Although the manager's responsibilities would be changed, they would still demand a standard of sensitivity and tact and a continuing man-manager relationship, which many would be hard put to meet. Not every employee would be willing to regard his immediate superior as a counselor in whom he should confide. For that matter, not every employee would be particularly interested in growth if it demanded effort and self-analysis. But that is precisely why it is so important to stimulate as many employees as possible to seek an enlargement of their competence. Management is constantly complaining that competence of all kinds, especially managerial competence, is in short supply. Surely part of the reason is that we do not suspect the potentiality for achievement until someone has begun to distinguish himself. Even if only a few people were recognized and stimulated to grow as a result of a counseling program, it would be well worth its cost.

It would be even more worthwhile from the employee's standpoint, with or without growth. A counseling program that provides a personal channel of upward communication, and that focuses managerial attention on *their* potentialities and desires, can be a powerful support to morale. It can be one of those "mighty intangibles" that make all the difference between a job that is just a job and one that is a rewarding experience in itself.

Careers

The counseling process is considerably more than a helpful gesture, and its purposes are much more practical than merely to win friends and influence employees. Its immediate goal is to enhance morale by responding to the concern that most people feel most of the time about their future. Its ultimate goal is to enlarge the company's supply of that chronically scarce commodity, highly developed talent.

Counseling is incapable of producing this result by itself, and it makes sense only in the context of personnel policies that are deliberately geared to match advances in competence with greater responsibilities and rewards. To introduce counseling in a static company that does not expect its employees to become capable of handling more difficult jobs than they already hold would be self-defeating; after a brief glow of hope it would lead to disillusionment. Therefore, the attempt to lift morale and assuage grievances by means of counseling is practical *only* when management is genuinely convinced that its employees can and should be developed to higher levels of competence. This premise, call it optimism or faith in human nature if you must,

is the sine qua non of an effective human relations program. Without it, apathy and passive resistance are likely to persist in the face of the most ardent efforts to counsel or communicate.

In this chapter, we will be concerned with the kinds of personnel programs that are addressed to the employee's future and (briefly) with the psychology that underlies them. The term *career planning* is a useful misnomer that can serve as a generic term for these programs. It is a misnomer because we cannot, as a practical matter, decide very far in advance what position a man should hold next. The "planning" in career planning is essentially a matter of seeing to it that appropriate positions are ready into which men can be moved when *they* are ready. Career planning is providing opportunities, not crystal-ball–gazing.

The Development Process

It should come as no surprise that the acquisition of competence, which usually proceeds at a fairly rapid rate during the school years, often slows down and even grinds to a halt during the early post-schooling phases of a man's career. As a student, the individual is not only faced by a formal educational apparatus designed to help him to learn, but also, more importantly, he is *motivated* to learn, even though this motivation is too often nipped in the bud as a result of unfortunate social conditions or inadequate educational methods. The point is: the school years are a period when the *motivation* to learn can be cultivated, if only advantage were taken of this opportunity.

The youthful motivation to learn is only partly due to the joy of mastering a subject or to the fear of failure. It is also due to the youth's situation. As the student becomes increasingly aware of the world, he is likely to recognize that he is in a position that allows for change and improvement. He has relatively little power or prestige, but it is quite possible to change all that through his own efforts. Indeed, given the pace of recent technological change, the avid student has a considerable advantage over all preceding graduates—an advantage that he may promptly lose to the future graduates who follow him. In any case, the student finds himself in a present made tolerable by a hopeful future, and it is this awareness of potential gain that makes him receptive to new ideas and information.

Before concluding this brief consideration of motivation, three observations should be added. First, this presentation has been an over-simplified version of how motivation actually operates, sufficient

for our purposes perhaps, but not really adequate to explain the process in any larger sense. Second, the gain the student anticipates in the future is not necessarily financial but rather an awareness that education provides an advantage in the quest for any kind of gain. Third, the optimistic frame of mind in which we have portrayed our hypothetical youth is a predominantly middle-class experience that tends, regrettably, to be stifled rather early in children who grow up in disadvantaged circumstances.

But the loss of motivation to learn is just as unfortunate, and just as unnecessary, when it occurs in a recent college graduate as when it occurs in a frustrated first-grader. Too often the process of acquiring a formal education is made into a drudgery from which the student is all too eager to escape, rather than an introduction to habits of inquiry and analysis that can last a lifetime. Too often the recent graduate who enters industry with an eagerness to question and discover becomes aware that these attitudes are not entirely welcome in an established organization. The result is worse than the much-lamented conformity of young employees, which is after all only the external symptom of a lack of motivation to learn. More serious is the growth of complacency —the attitude that problems will eventually solve themselves if ignored long enough—and the growth of the attitude that existing methods could not have survived this long if they hadn't been superior to all others. The failure of many employees to persistently enlarge their competence after completing their formal education is a severe handicap to the organizations that employ them.

The reason why some organizations grow and prosper is that *enough* individuals within them manage to escape this dreary cycle of learning not to learn. Many companies have personnel development programs that are intended to encourage such an escape. These take various forms, but it is important to realize that the subject matter and content of these programs have only a secondary importance. Their primary impact, if they have an impact at all, is motivational. What is taught in the typical development program is less important than whether the individual's *curiosity* can be reignited. The kind of learning that characterizes real development (or if you will, real enlargement of competence) is an active personal attempt to make sense of the job environment in one's own terms. It is not the simple memorizing or parroting that occurs in some classrooms. In this sense, all meaningful development is self-development, and all "developed" men are self-made.

We don't really know very much about why some men grow wiser and broader in their perspective, while others gain little from their experiences. It seems clear that while development can sometimes be stimulated through formal programs, it cannot be produced by simply running enough people through a sufficiently elaborate program. But since most learning occurs on the job rather than in the development program, it follows that the internal environment of the organization has a great deal to do with how often, and how far, the development process will occur.

Promotion

One of the most important aspects of the organization's environment is its promotion system, which can be thought of as a way of taking official notice that some kind of growth has occurred. The potency of promotion as a motivator is due to two factors. First, it is addressed to the future and therefore is especially interesting to younger people, who are sensitive to any indication of what may be in store for them. Second, a promotion is one of the few organizational rewards that affects one's standing in the external social environment.

The administration of an effective promotion program is a demanding and complex exercise in human relations. Where so many egos are exposed to potential abrasions, some kind of compromise is necessary between an utterly objective appraisal of performance and the dignity of those who have been appraised. The problem is to keep to the middle of the road. The wise manager does not promote people automatically, and nor does he promote them without considerable regard for the consequences.

Promotions into management or other highly responsible positions present a particularly difficult problem. In companies that stress promotion as the principal means of recognizing superior performance, there is a tendency for unpromoted employees to look upon managerial status as a reward they are being denied. To feel that promotions are being distributed unfairly to friends of management, or to people who manage to make themselves conspicuous, is a common rationalization among such people. It is harmless to the extent that they simply use it to make their status more tolerable; when there is any truth to such feelings the consequences for morale can be quite serious. Sometimes, companies are so leery of letting this situation occur that they swing to the opposite extreme and promote according

to job seniority or total length of service. This exonerates management from any suspicion of favoritism, but it also produces little incentive for capable employees to distinguish themselves.

Many companies pride themselves on promoting strictly according to merit, but a merit promotion system that is not tempered by a recognition of human realities is unworkable. A strictly merit system would operate the management structure somewhat like a "hotel", that is, every management position is regarded as a "room" in which each managerial "guest" is accommodated until the next "guest" arrives. The management structure endures, but its human tenants are temporary. When companies have attempted to operate in this way, they have usually regretted it. While no job should be regarded as the property of its incumbent, a strict merit policy can damage the dignity of those involved so severely that the gain is hardly worth the cost. It is for this reason that a number of face-saving devices have been developed. Among these are the assignment of men to jobs that match the titles and perquisites, but not the responsibilities, of their previous jobs; and permitting a man to remain in his job while dividing several of his responsibilities among peers or assistants.

Promotion almost always implies an increase in managerial authority or responsibility. This has the effect of denying promotion to men who, while they may neither aspire to nor qualify for being someone else's boss, have acquired a high degree of technical expertise. In organizations that are heavily research-oriented, or that require a high degree of technical skill, this kind of promotion policy can cause serious morale problems. It is not so much a matter of everyone wanting to be a manager as of a feeling that recognition is being denied to those on whose efforts the company ultimately depends. To correct this problem, some companies have introduced so-called dual ladder or parallel track promotion systems. These provide for a conventional promotion channel into supervisory and management positions and a new channel into positions of increased technical or professional responsibility. The second channel roughly matches the first with regard to titles, perquisites, and pay. The main difference is in the assignments themselves. Dual ladder systems do not always work successfully. When they do not, it is usually because of either of two reasons: Either they fail to provide meaningful upgrading in technical responsibilities ("I've got a fancy title now, but I'm doing the same old job"), or they have a tendency to provide more recognition (or more conspicuous recognition) to men who are promoted through the managerial channel than to those who are promoted through the technical channel.

Personnel Planning

One of the main responsibilities of personnel management is to anticipate the company's personnel requirements far enough in advance to assure that an adequate supply of qualified people are available to fill the right jobs at the right times. In companies that are heavily involved in technological change, this often means an almost constant redistribution of talent from obsolescent skills to newer skills that may be almost unheard of when the planning begins.

Personnel planners are of course concerned with new hires and with attrition. For our purposes, we will concentrate on their involvement with the careers of employees who may be expected to remain in the firm for some time. Unless a company is in an unusually rapid expansion phase, the bulk of its work in the foreseeable future will undoubtedly be done by existing employees. The foreseeable future of today's personnel is thus the major concern of personnel planners. What must be done in this type of planning, if it is to be effective, is to subtly blend hardheaded forecasting with sensitivity to human aspirations and peculiarities. The objective is to place people not only where they will be needed, but also where they will be glad to be. Sophisticated personnel planning attempts to build motivation into tomorrow's assignments or at least to avoid unnecessary boredom and frustration. This requires an understanding of attitudes toward tenure in assignments. Although there is no standard attitude, a number of typical ones may be described. Each calls for a somewhat different approach.

First, among younger men or ambitious men of all ages there is a tendency to be content to remain in a given job only as long as it seems to be contributing to their preparation for more demanding jobs. Once such a man feels he has mastered a given assignment, it is usually a mistake to keep him in it for too long. He will either lose his enthusiasm or seek another employer. Even liberal remuneration will provide only temporary reconciliation to such a situation. To keep such men highly motivated, it is wise to provide reassignments every few years.

There is a quite different and very common attitude toward changes of assignment found in men who no longer aspire to greater challenges, or who never did. Such men want to stay where they are. If possible, they also want their jobs to keep their position in the status hierarchy relative to other jobs. For this reason, they tend to belittle or disparage jobs that begin to assume greater importance than

theirs for technological or organizational reasons. Sometimes they are not above a little subtle sabotage, in the form of concealing information or providing slow service when one of the competing departments requires their cooperation. While such people prefer not to be exposed to change, they seldom want to be taken for granted. They tend to be quite appreciative of paternalistic gestures by management, and they are quite sensitive to the merest suggestion that their loyalty and contributions to the firm may no longer be quite as valued as they once were. Consequently, the wise administrator plans a more or less constant program of small but meaningful gestures toward such employees to show that they are still appreciated, but he tries to minimize the demands made upon them for change.

Another particularly difficult human relations problem is posed by the individual whose estimate of his own accomplishments greatly exceeds everyone else's. Such people find it difficult to understand why their potentialities are being overlooked, and they may go to considerable lengths to bring themselves to the attention of someone who is in a position to do something about it. Their persistence and earnestness may deter managers from explaining their deficiencies with the necessary bluntness. As a result, these individuals tend to become frustrated and bewildered by their failure to be recognized.

In the end, no matter how large the organization and no matter how many new positions are being set up for future use, personnel planning must be applied to individuals. For this reason it is essential that personnel planners have access to information about the way in which employees are expanding their job competence, their interest in other kinds of assignments, and their ability to absorb new knowledge and to acquire new skills. The best source of this kind of information is an admittedly fallible one: the first-line supervisor. This is another reason why it is so important that supervisors be trained to evaluate the performance of their employees as objectively as possible, and why their recorded performance appraisals constitute such a vital input to effective personnel planning.

Retraining

It has been said that a young man beginning his career today should be prepared to change his *career field* at least three times before he retires, and perhaps even more often. This is because of the tendency of traditional skills to become obsolete. For this reason, industry is making an increasingly heavy annual investment in retraining its own personnel.

Retraining may include periodic refresher courses, updating courses that introduce recent developments, or wholly new material dealing with new products or processes. In this section we will consider some of the problems that are involved in effective retraining and some of its interesting side-effects.

Men who have not been in classrooms for years tend to regard retraining with a certain amount of trepidation. This is partly because they may have grown unaccustomed to the learning process or to the study process. There is also the fear of not performing well, especially in comparison with younger employees whose study habits have had less time to weaken. A wisely designed retraining program can help the older employee counteract both real and imagined disadvantages.

Real learning disadvantages in retraining tend to be of three main sorts: the necessity to unlearn obsolete habits and ideas, basic educational handicaps, and increasing aptitude requirements. Regarding unlearning, it sometimes happens that an old, well-learned skill competes with a newer one, in the sense that the old habits keep appearing even though they are no longer appropriate. This is what happens, for example, when a driver who is accustomed to a standard gearshift begins to drive a car with an automatic shift, and continues to reach for a nonexistant clutch pedal. In general, whenever the old and the new skills involve differing approaches to similar operations, the problem of ridding the student of inappropriate, ingrained habits is likely to occur. It is by no means insurmountable, but time and patience are required to solve it.

Basic educational handicaps are more serious. Many older employees began their careers at a time when educational standards were much lower than they are today. A little more than a generation ago, a high school graduate was considered to be an unusually well-educated man. Today's high school graduate, although he has had a much better exposure to the sciences and other subjects than the graduate of a generation ago, is considered to have met only the minimum standard for entry into the labor market. Older employees are thus quite disadvantaged in terms of basic educational skills. In addition, many younger workers who failed to complete high school or who went through inadequate educational programs are also handicapped. Whether young or old, people who lack a sufficient fund of basic knowledge find it very difficult to absorb new skills when these are based on an understanding of the very concepts they lack.

This point was clearly illustrated by a study in the main plant of a large east coast manufacturer. This plant was being converted from the manufacture of relatively simple mechanical devices to much

more complex electronic devices. In the course of retraining the workers to deal with electronics manufacturing, the company found that its older employees were not doing nearly as well as the younger ones. Rather than simply accept the obvious conclusion that age somehow made men deficient in their ability to learn, the company decided on an experiment. Reasoning that the older men did not have as adequate an educational background as the younger ones, the company organized a special pre-retraining "cram" course for the older men. For several weeks they were given intensive instruction in such subjects as high school algebra and physics. Then they entered the regular electronics retraining program along with a group of younger men. The older group acquitted itself quite well and proved again that learning ability does not necessarily atrophy with age.

Changing aptitude requirements pose a still more difficult problem for retraining. On the one hand, training directors are faced with the necessity of supplying a corporation with large numbers of employees who are qualified to work in new, sometimes spectacularly new, technologies. These directors have an understandable tendency to overestimate the aptitude requirements of these new jobs. It is better, after all, to err on the side of caution; until the real aptitude requirements of a new job can be established empirically, most companies tend to assign them to overqualified employees. This makes for boredom among the selected men and frustration among the unselected ones. On the other hand, as some jobs evolve toward higher levels of sophistication they tend to require a degree of acumen and understanding that was previously unnecessary. This tends to happen in sales and maintenance organizations when the product being sold or serviced becomes more complex. Sometimes the retraining problem can be dealt with by means of extended "*hands-on*" training, but it is sometimes necessary to reassign such men to less demanding jobs. This frequently causes a loss of prestige and morale. Consequently, men whose jobs outgrow them through no fault of their own should be assigned to the most challenging and responsible jobs they can handle. They should not be relegated to menial or contrived jobs.

It should be noted that when a company is heavily committed to an employee retraining program, attendance at its courses tends to take on the connotations of a status symbol. The first group to be retrained is usually regarded as the special favorites of management by the other employees. Those who have not yet been assigned to classes after the program has been in effect for a while become anxious and

tend to feel rejected. Therefore, a company embarking on a retraining program should make its intentions clear at the outset to all affected employees.

Retirement

It is now recognized that both employer and employee have an important stake in effective preparation for retirement. From the company's standpoint, a sound preretirement program assures that the employee's last few years on the job will be productive, rather than a costly matter of coasting downhill. It also assures that the morale of younger employees will not be adversely affected by the complaints of disgruntled older men who feel that they are being denied an opportunity to continue in their accustomed job roles. From the employee's standpoint, a retirement planning program can help to preserve his self-respect while removing some of the dread of having no job, and having to live on a reduced income. It is a fact that while men often grouse about their jobs, they also become dependent on them for a sense of purpose and of being wanted. To be suddenly deprived of these supports, even when financial security is provided, can be a serious blow to a man's morale.

As life expectancies lengthen and more and more men reach retirement age, adjustment problems are becoming increasingly common. Most companies and unions now provide pension plans that at least assure that the retired worker can maintain an acceptable standard of living, even if the scale is reduced from what he may have enjoyed during his peak earning years. But it is more difficult to assure that the retired man will find life meaningful. The frequency of psychosomatic disorders among newly retired men attests that many do not adjust well to their new situation.

The two most important ingredients of a successful retirement policy are flexibility on the part of the company and preparation on the part of the individual. Unfortunately, most retirement plans still insist rigidly that all employees will be retired when they reach a particular age, usually 65. This fails to recognize the fact that men differ widely in their readiness for retirement. Some pass the peak of their productivity in their thirties or forties and then make only a marginal (or worse) contribution to their companies for upwards of twenty more years. Others reach 65 in full possession of their energy and acumen, and they are quite able to go on making a substantial contribu-

tion for many more years. Due to improving health and educational standards, there is reason to expect that this type of older employee will become increasingly common in the future.

Some retirement plans recognize the variability of retirement needs by providing both early retirement (which is usually available from about age 55 onward, with a reduced pension rate), and the option of continued employment beyond 65 if this is mutually desired by both parties. While these plans are not necessarily easy to administer, they have the advantages of maximum utilization of the employee's productive years and maximum choice on the part of the individual regarding how his later years will be spent.

Preparation for retirement usually involves discussions between the employee and a counselor. This counseling may begin as much as five years before the anticipated retirement date. These discussions are designed to provide the employee with financial data and other facts that would be pertinent to his retirement planning. They are also designed to help the employee begin advance planning for retirement so he has plenty of time to decide where he would like to live, how to spend his time, whether and how to supplement his income, and so on. Perhaps the most important aspect of preparation for retirement, however, concerns the employee's last few job assignments. Whenever possible, it is desirable to give him assignments that fully utilize his abilities right down to retirement day itself. This practice sends the man into retirement with a sense of adequacy that only the demonstrated respect of his employer and fellow-employees can bring. Testimonial dinners and gold watches are no substitute for a company's acknowledged desire to keep a man in the job he does best for as long as possible.

Unfortunately, this doesn't happen as often as it should. Too frequently, older employees are assigned to relatively undemanding or unimportant jobs. Even when there is no loss in pay, the clear implication that the employee is no longer able to maintain his former proficiency cannot fail to hurt. Sometimes this procedure is followed to make room for younger men. Sometimes this action reflects a belief that the older employee would prefer to spend his remaining working days as comfortably as possible. Sometimes it is based on the assumption that the older employee is incapable of learning a new job when his old one becomes obsolete. While any of these reasons may be valid in individual cases, it is a serious mistake to assume that they apply in all instances.

The adjustment to retirement may be difficult or easy, depending

on whether or not the individual has developed alternative activities to provide an outlet for his energies and talents. The man with well-developed interests or hobbies enters retirement with a decided advantage over the man who has been wedded to his job and whose leisure time has consisted largely of resting from his job. There are many activities open to the retired person other than puttering around and hobbies: community service, study, consulting, part-time work of various kinds. Which of these is most appropriate can only be determined by the individual himself. Part of the rationale of retirement counseling, of course, is to introduce the employee to these problems some time before actual retirement and to start him thinking about them early. Some companies even provide extensive vacations, often up to six months, in the years prior to retirement, to give the employee a chance to actually experiment with various forms of retirement activity.

There are two problems related to retirement whose importance we are only beginning to discern and for which we have as yet no satisfactory solution. One is the question of whether mandatory retirement is really justified. The other is the tendency of most pension plans to "lock in" an employee to his particular company, even though it may be in the best interests of everyone for him to accept a new job elsewhere.

Retirement, like many other institutions established on premises that have since altered, needs to be adapted to the changing times. At one time, life expectancies for working people were such that relatively few actually reached the age of retirement. Today most workers will. At one time, most jobs consisted of an unrewarding drudgery from which any form of release would be only too welcome. Today a great many jobs exist that actually challenge and absorb the individual for years. At one time, most men were educated only to the rudimentary level required by their jobs, and their interest in their work proceeded only as far as their understanding. Today many men are able to appreciate, and are stimulated by, the wider ramifications of their work. The result of these changes is that an increasing number of men arrive at retirement age full of zest and undiminished abilities that their companies would be hard put to replace. It is because of this trend that some of our old, unexamined assumptions about retirement, such as the idea that it is wrong to permit a man to continue working beyond a certain age, need to be questioned seriously.

A long-service employee in a company with a good pension plan gradually finds it contrary to his best financial interests to consider

leaving that company. This, of course, is one of the things a pension plan is designed to do. The employee who elects to leave such a company usually enters the plan of his next employer at a considerable loss in potential pension benefits. Some plans provide for a vested interest in a part of the pension rights if service is continued beyond a specified period, but even so a financial penalty is ultimately incurred if the employee elects to leave. The consequences of these plans are not always healthy for the individual or the company. The employee, especially in managerial, professional or technical jobs, may find himself financially committed to a company that cannot offer him as stimulating, prestigeful, or remunerative a job (in terms of immediate earnings) as another company. His employer, on the other hand, may find himself unable to utilize his abilities in an efficient and satisfactory way. This situation is likely to generate grumbling and discontent that may easily spread to other employees.

While a high turnover rate represents a cost to be avoided if possible, a moderate amount of turnover can be healthy. It provides an outlet for otherwise insoluble frustrations and provides alternative pathways for employees who find themselves dissatisfied with the opportunities available to them. It is not in the company's interest to bind either type of employee to it with pension considerations alone. If the problem cannot be solved at the level of the job itself, it may be best on balance to let the connection be severed. Some ways of accomplishing this are currently being developed. In the "portable pension" approach, the employee's accrued pension funds transfer from one employer to another. Various forms of early vesting, which guarantee at least a part of the pension regardless of whether or not the employee stays with his company, are also in use. But these experimental solutions have not been fully tested. Until and unless a more comprehensive answer is found, the human relations problems that result from employees' immobilization by pension rights will continue to plague both employers and employees alike.

Human Relations Problems

When managers speak of human relations problems, they are usually using a euphemism for describing people who may be angry, disappointed, frightened, or hostile—for people, in other words, whose emotions are showing. At one time or another anyone can be provoked beyond the limits of his normal reserve, and for some people those limits are reached fairly often. Inevitably, therefore, management finds it necessary to deal with people at various levels of emotional distress.

There are three basic objectives in dealing with any human relations problem, and none of them is easy to reach. The first is to confine the problem so that it affects as few people, and causes as little interruption of work, as possible. The second is to reach a just settlement within the framework of company policy, union contracts or local tradition, or both. The third is to leave the relationship between the affected parties viable, that is, to permit them all to continue working together with a reasonable degree of harmony. The main reason why all of these goals are hard to reach is that managers, being human, are neither entirely objective nor above being swayed by

their own anger, disappointment, and so on. Most of the problems that management has to deal with are triggered by relatively small events, and the individual's reaction to the situation may seem quite disproportionate to its apparent cause. For this reason, some managers have a tendency to assume that the employee who allows himself to become upset is either a chronic malcontent or a good man having a bad day. Such conclusions are quite unfortunate, because they prevent the manager from investigating, and therefore from understanding, what could be a serious underlying situation.

The problems that most people have at work, when they have them at all, are usually symptoms of something larger. That is, an employee seldom becomes discontented suddenly or capriciously: he is likely to endure some festering complaint for a long time until finally some incident provokes an overt display of emotion. The wise manager realizes that whatever provoked the reaction is not nearly as important as what undermined the employee's ability to resist provocation. The manager also realizes that when one man has reached his boiling point, there are likely to be many others in various stages of overheating whose attitudes have not yet become obvious. Once a problem has erupted, there is seldom any painless way to ease the situation. Any overt confrontation leaves scars, and sometimes the tensions they create are insoluble. An ounce of the kind of managerial sensitivity that can anticipate and prevent a human relations problem is worth a pound of the kind of managerial finesse that can alleviate or pacify an uncomfortable incident once it has occurred.

We have already discussed at some length the kinds of long-term stresses that can build up and eventually make the employee susceptible to open discontent. Among these, arbitrary supervision, inadequate communication, and poor career planning are perhaps the most important. To this list might be added discrimination (whether real or apparent) between employees, lack of job security, inadequate or inequitable pay, and prolonged exposure to undesirable conditions (such as second shifts). Any perceptive manager is continually on the alert for any of these conditions, or even for a suggestion of them, because he knows they can erode morale if they persist. However, some individual problems will occur despite the utmost vigilance, and handling them sensibly can be a severe challenge to management.

In this chapter we will be concerned with some of the more common problems that can occur between managers and employees and with some principles that can be helpful in dealing with them. It

should be understood at the outset, however, that there can be no such thing as a simple "cookbook" approach to solving human relations problems. The best advice the manager can expect to receive is that he should try very hard to understand the employee's point of view. Beyond that, the manager's best guide is his own sense of what is fair and what is practical.

Absenteeism and Tardiness

Absenteeism and tardiness are problems that management *cannot* ignore, even if it has weightier matters to attend to, and it almost certainly has. The productivity of many jobs is largely a matter of the amount of time the employee spends working at them. One obvious example is the typist, who, by arriving for work fifteen minutes late, decreases her output by one letter; or by not arriving at all on a given day decreases her productivity for the week by about 20 percent. In companies having a high proportion of jobs in which productivity is closely correlated with time spent at work, absenteeism and tardiness can add a substantial burden to operating costs.

The real cost of these problems, however, is greater, and harder to measure, than a simple matter of letters not written or of work falling behind schedule. To understand why this is so, one must first draw a distinction between occasional and habitual absences (or latenesses). It is obviously impossible for every employee to report to work on time every day. Given the vicissitudes of commuting, the weather, and the common cold, it is not reasonable to expect it. But it is one thing to recognize that anyone can be late or absent from time to time and quite another to countenance their doing so regularly. No one knows better who is making a habit of absences, or of latenesses, than the employee in the same department who makes it his business to get to work on time. In other words, any implication that the guilty are getting the same treatment as the innocent will cause resentment among the innocent. This can lead to anything from simple grumbling to a general deterioration of discipline. More subtly, it can lead to carelessness and complacency as employees become convinced that management doesn't really care about how they conduct themselves. Whether toleration of lateness and absenteeism leads to minor or major consequences depends on other factors, such as the general state of morale and the company's labor-relations history. The point is that habitual lateness and absenteeism create an exposure to conse-

quences that are far more serious than these problems themselves. To permit them to go unchecked is, in a way, like allowing a dike to fall into disrepair.

The immediate reasons for habitual lateness are the same as for the occasional variety. They are usually trivial and can be anything from a traffic delay to a barely-missed train or bus to five extra minutes in bed. The cure is usually a simple matter of leaving for work early enough to be able to offset most delays. As a rule, the habitually late employee does not attempt to do this, either because he has never developed the habit of promptness or because he thinks it is unimportant. In some cases, he simply dislikes his job and is reluctant to go to it at all. To the extent that habitual lateness is simply a bad habit, continued firmness on the part of management will usually be an adequate corrective device. To the extent that it has deeper causes, it may require counseling or even the severing of a mutually unsatisfactory work relationship.

Habitual absence is more complex. Sometimes it is due to a legitimate medical problem, in which case special arrangements can usually be worked out to help the employee to recover or to adapt his job to his limitations. Sometimes, however, it will be due to the employee's not *wanting* to go to work. He may prefer a day of recreation, shopping, or looking for another job. This type of abuse is easy to suspect but difficult to prove. Again, a firm insistence by management on an adequate attendance record can eliminate most of these absences; where this approach fails, more severe measures may be necessary.

Some interesting problems have arisen in industry as an indirect result of statutes regarding the recording of and payment for overtime work. Even though they benefit financially from these provisions, nonexempt employees (those who must receive additional compensation for overtime) tend to regard the act of recording their worktime as a sort of negative status symbol. This is especially true when employees in the higher-paid exempt positions are not required to record their time. Attempts to alleviate these feelings of discrimination by requiring all employees to record their worktime usually backfire. This occurs because exempt employees are, if anything, even more sensitive to the status implications of time recording than those who are required to fill out time sheets. The problem is in one sense only minor, since most people can bear time recording well enough even though they may grumble about it. When the grumbling rises in intensity, it is usually an indirect reflection of dissatisfaction in a less

tangible, less easily expressed area. Some companies are experimenting with having each employee record his own worktime privately, on the honor system, but whether this is an adequate solution remains to be seen. Meanwhile, the problem of how to assuage feelings while assuring that employees are properly paid, and that the law is complied with, still plagues personnel managers.

Denying Requests

One of the most common, and therefore the least analyzed, problems of everyday management is that of having to turn down an employee's request for some favor or benefit. These requests may range in importance all the way from wanting to leave a few minutes early one day to wanting a promotion.

The most important thing for the manager to remember about any employee request is that the employee considers it important, otherwise he wouldn't have made it. Even requests that may seem trivial or frivolous should not be lightly dismissed, especially when the manager is unlikely to appreciate the employee's values. This may occur, for example, when the manager is considerably older than the employee, or when an older male is supervising young female employees. A corollary of taking all requests seriously is remembering them. Most people do not like to pester their superiors with repeated questions. They prefer to ask once and get an answer without having to remind him that they have asked. Unfortunately, some supervisors assume that an employee who does not repeat a request has forgotten about it and that the supervisor should do likewise. But this only leads to grudges, to feelings of being ignored or taken for granted. The result is a conviction that requests should not be taken to the supervisor at all but rather to some higher authority or to an outsider.

Many requests have to be denied, and it is important that this be done not only for sufficient reasons but also in such a way that the employee *recognizes* the reasons to be sufficient. Consequently, it is seldom wise to reject a request without taking time to consider it carefully. A summary rejection implies that the employee's case has not had a fair hearing. Therefore, unless the request is essentially identical to one the same individual has already been refused, or unless the request is for an action that must be taken quickly if at all, it is best to take it under advisement before making a decision. A corollary of not rejecting a request summarily is not rejecting it at all if it is possible to justify it. Too many supervisors operate on the premise

that it is their job to prevent *any* deviation from normal routine. This is of course an absurd attitude. But it is equally foolish to permit exceptions that create dissension. Unless a privilege is available to *all* employees under clearly definable conditions, it is unwise to grant it to one man. Precedent-setting decisions are perhaps the stickiest everyday problem faced by first-line managers.

A request that has been promised a reply deserves a reasonably prompt answer. It is one thing to review a request and quite another to deliberate at too great length. In fact, there is something to be said for promising, at the time a request is received, that a decision will be reached by a specified day, preferably within 24 hours. When a request is denied, the reason for the denial must be clearly stated. It damages morale severely to deny something without an explanation, but it is nearly as bad to be given an unconvincing reason. Some classically unconvincing reasons that a smart supervisor would never use are: "It's against company policy," "We've never done it before," and "I just don't think it's a good idea."

Inadequate Performance

The classical solution to the problem of the employee whose productivity was too low, or whose attitude was too troublesome, was simply to fire him and be done with it. Today it is no longer as easy to dismiss employees as it once was, and neither is this practice always regarded as being the best possible solution. One reason for this change has been the growth of rationalized methods of personnel selection, which are designed to prevent the hiring of potentially unqualified employees. Although selection and placement is by no means an exact science, a soundly developed staffing program can greatly reduce turnover due to incompetence, unreliability, or untrainability.

Another reason for the decline in summary dismissals has been the growth of labor unions, which not only protect their own members from firing, but indirectly affect the practices of firms that are not unionized and are eager to remain that way. Further, economic growth itself has discouraged firing by creating labor shortages in many occupations. In a tight labor market, most firms prefer marginal personnel to none at all; few are willing to mar their image (that is, their ability to attract qualified new hires) by needlessly acquiring a reputation for firing.

For all of these reasons, it is increasingly common to try to sal-

vage the inadequate performer, if possible; and even to find ways of continuing to "carry" the employee who is unable to pull his own weight. Dismissal still exists, of course, but it is used more and more as a last resort rather than as a simple expedient.

In the attempt to salvage the faltering employee, or in arranging the departure of one who could not be salvaged, it is of the utmost importance that the individual understand what is happening and why. This is most difficult to bring about. Managers frequently prefer to suffer an inadequate employee in silence, or to express their dissatisfaction in muted, indirect terms, rather than tell him bluntly what is wrong. Partly as a result of such delicacy, the employee whose work is unsatisfactory often feels that he is not in serious trouble. The longer such a situation persists, the harder it becomes to resolve it. Should he finally be dismissed, the employee will regard it as sudden and unjust. He will in fact have every right to feel that way, even if his work has actually been unsatisfactory for years. Further, the incident is likely to be embroidered and enlarged upon as it passes through sympathetic and uninformed hands, so that in the end the company's reputation for fairness will suffer badly.

It is perhaps too optimistic to expect that all separations can be accomplished on the basis of mutual consent. But this should always be the objective, and in well-managed companies it can frequently be achieved. The decision to separate an individual should never be arrived at lightly, and the reasons for it should be abundantly clear to all parties. Further, it should be equally clear that all reasonable alternatives, such as reassignment, retraining, or the inevitable "second chance," have either been tried or are not feasible. Many problems of inadequate performance are cleared up quite satisfactorily by a scrupulous adherence to the principle of trying all other alternatives before resorting to discharge. This is especially true when the difficulty was due to carelessness or complacency on the employee's part (an unmistakable warning will often suffice to snap him out of his lethargy), or to incompatibility between the supervisor and the employee (in which case a simple reassignment sometimes works wonders). In general, it is to everyone's advantage to make the process of involuntary separation as hard to resort to as possible.

However, there is an enormous difference between trying to retain potentially productive employees and simply tolerating unproductive employees. If the latter situation persists long enough, the individual becomes, in a moral if not in a legal sense, "unfirable." He can claim with some justice that he has served the company faithfully

during the years when it would have been far easier for him to find another job than it would be now. Further, the company's failure to indicate its dissatisfaction during those years would seem to have implicitly encouraged him to stay in its employ, performing at the level that only now are they questioning. Consequently, the key to effective management of inadequate performance is frankness. The longer management avoids facing the issue, the less manageable it becomes.

Firing

During World War II, when feelings were running understandably high, the late Sir Winston Churchill was criticized for the courtesy and correctness with which he informed the Japanese Ambassador that Britain was at war with Japan. Churchill's rejoinder was, "After all, when you have to kill a man it costs nothing to be polite." The same is true of firing, which is undoubtedly the sorriest and most traumatic experience in industrial relations for managers and employees alike. Precisely because it is so painful, it tends to be badly handled: by procrastination, a mutual failure to communicate, or by precipitate and often clumsy action. Since the necessity of involuntarily separating an employee from his job will undoubtedly continue to occur, there is much to be gained from learning to handle it with greater finesse.

Human nature being what it is, managers may tend to view a dismissal as overdue and richly deserved, while employees tend to view it as unjust and malicious. Even when alternative jobs are plentiful, working people resent being fired because it implies inadequacy on their part and because it forces a major change upon them without their consent. When other jobs are scarce, an economic penalty is added to the psychological one. Therefore, the motivation to prevent firing, or at least to make it difficult to utilize, is extremely strong. This is why employment security is at the heart of most union contracts.

Whether because of contracts or custom, employees in many organizations tend to become "unfirable" after they have completed a certain period of service. The term has to be put between quotation marks, because it is not literally true, and only unwritten policy tends to support it. On the other hand, involuntary separations of seasoned employees tend to be very rare. This leads mainly to loyalty, but it can also cause complacency. There are times when mere length of service does not suffice to prevent firing. Corporate mergers, changes

of management, or severe profit squeezes in previously prosperous companies can all dispel the usual protection. Further, the new and unproven employee is traditionally in an exposed position until he can demonstrate his worth, and sometimes he cannot. Management therefore finds itself from time to time in the position of letting people go who do not want to be let go.

Broadly speaking, there are four major considerations in any involuntary separation. The first is ascertaining that the action is indeed necessary and that all other reasonable alternatives have ben exhausted. Unless an immediate separation is compelled by some gross violation, such as theft or malicious destruction of property, the employee should have been given ample warning and a clear indication of what was lacking in his performance and a reasonable chance to correct his deficiencies. Sometimes, management tends to become preoccupied with building its case, that is, with documenting the employee's shortcomings in order to refute any protests that might be made. This is often a wise precaution, but the employee should still be advised of the precise reasons for management's dissatisfaction. Ideally, every separated employee should be fully aware of the events leading to the decision as they occurred and should agree that it is in his as well as the company's best interests that he leave. But in real life that is a great deal to expect. After all, if he were really convinced that he would be better off elsewhere he would presumably have taken steps to accomplish that already. Most involuntary separations are quite involuntary; hence the need for taking every reasonably step to demonstrate to the employee that he is being dealt with fairly.

The second major consideration concerns the employee's next job. It has not been traditional for employers to take any responsibility for post-termination placement beyond providing references, but there is increasing recognition of an obligation to help. In some cases this consists of severance pay liberal enough to sustain the former employee during a job search; in others it consists of time off at full pay for interviews with prospective employers while the individual is still on the first company's payroll. Some companies provide a counseling service to those individuals who are willing to take advantage of it; others actually try to place their former employees with other companies. (The latter is done mainly when a plant has been shut down, but it is not unheard of for this to happen when the company feels a special obligation to the separated employee.)

The third major consideration is the fired employee's need for a

chance to vent his emotions. Even with the most careful handling, an employee who has lost his job is likely to feel angry and frustrated. When he has been dealt with in a less-than-cautious way he may feel very bitter indeed. It is not generally recognized how powerful these feelings can be; many men are at least temporarily immobilized by them. At a time when they should be assessing their situation in a cool, clear manner, they may be consumed with resentment, wounded pride, and just plain fury. The experience of being fired, in other words, often renders a man incapable of doing anything about it.

In time, of course, most men get over their anger. But time is what most fired men can least afford to waste. They need to work their way through their emotions and back to a fairly steady state of mind as quickly as possible. In most cases, this cannot be done very effectively by exhorting them to get hold of themselves. It is better to let the storm blow itself out than to try to supress it. This is the principle underlying the clinics for recently fired men that are being organized on an experimental basis in certain cities. This program (which is partly supported by the former employer and partly by the participants) is designed to bring the individual's normal feelings of hostility to the surface fairly quickly and in a safe, understanding environment. As soon as he has vented enough feeling to be able to get some perspective on himself, and to recognize that however justified his anger may be it is irrelevant and useless in his present situation, he is ready to cooperate in a systematic search for the best available employment.

It is easy to scoff at such programs as a sort of poor man's psychoanalysis. They are nothing of the kind. They have about the same relationship to psychoanalysis that first aid has to surgery. But these programs *do* permit the fired employee with a normal case of frustration to come to grips with his real problems more quickly than he probably could by himself. Others can achieve the same result without the formalities of a program through consultation with a wise and sympathetic supervisor, and understanding wife, or a good friend. What is new in these programs is the recognition that firing does a certain amount of psychological damage that should be repaired as quickly as possible, and the recognition that the former employer should help in some way to accomplish that repair.

The fourth important consideration in firing concerns the reaction of remaining employees, who can hardly avoid being curious and apprehensive when one of their number is dismissed. Here management often finds itself in a dilemma. To disclose the details behind the

decision to fire a man would often persuade other employees that it was a just move that need not arouse their fears. But it might also be disclosing confidential information that is none of the other employees', or anyone else's, business. In practice, therefore, most separations take place within a certain cloak of secrecy that preserves decency but also raises anxieties. Very few employees would object to management's firing someone for just and adequate reasons. They might quibble over what constitutes just and adequate reasons, and when none are given they may suspect that management is accomplishing its own purposes at the expense of innocent employees. There is really *no* adequate way out of this dilemma. Therefore, management's best strategy is not to get into it in the first place. This can be done generally by cultivating a good human relations climate and more specifically by giving the inadequate employee every reasonable assistance and consideration before taking the last irrevocable step.

This discussion of involuntary separation has assumed, of course, that it is possible to dismiss employees. In some companies union contracts may make firing, for all practical purposes, impossible. Even so, management is not entirely without recourse in dealing with unsatisfactory employees, even if that recourse consists only in withholding some small favor or recognition. But regardless of whether the company exercises a free or a restricted hand in dealing with inadequate performers, the principles of effective management are the same. Once a company agrees to hire a man, it owes him a reasonable opportunity to prove, and if necessary to reprove, that he deserves to remain employed permanently.

Morale

Morale is difficult to define or measure, and like physical health it is something we sense acutely only when it is in poor shape. Yet there are times when it has an almost palpable reality. Even when it does not command our attention, it is linked in subtle ways to the results an organization can achieve. When the term "morale" is used collectively, it refers to the working climate or atmosphere generated by the combined attitudes of a group of people toward their jobs. When it is used individually, it usually refers to the degree of satisfaction, optimism, and security—or the lack of these—that a particular person feels in connection with his job. Either way it is a highly intangible and subjective concept. For all its evanescence, morale is vital. It is the difference between outstanding performance and ordinary performance, between taking adversity in stride and collapsing, between a smoothly meshing organization and one that is continuously at odds with itself. Morale, like physical health, is the sum and result of many interrelated systems: it is a sort of summary of the condition of human relations in a particular group or person.

This chapter will first discuss some of the ways in which good

and poor morale may be recognized, and some of the consequences of both. It will then consider the nature of morale change, and some of the methods by which morale can be measured. It will close with a review of employee opinion survey programs and action programs that should accompany them.

It is sometimes assumed that when the morale of a group of employees is very good, they will show this by overt enthusiasm, or by emphatic expressions of satisfaction, or by zealous work performance. Similarly, it is assumed that when morale is poor, employees will show it by grumbling, uncooperativeness, and possibly by agitation against their employers. Actually neither of these assumptions is very accurate. Both are extremes that are rarely reached and usually only briefly maintained. If morale is thought of as a fluctuating or variable process that can move upward or downward along a continuum, then employee morale is usually found well inward from both extremes.

It is important to distinguish between the *causes, symptoms,* and *effects* of morale. Broadly speaking, most morale conditions are caused by management policies and practices, although they are also influenced by external conditions such as the history of labor-management relations in a given region.

The symptoms of morale are the readily observable forms of employee behavior that tend to reflect an underlying morale condition. These symptoms are best regarded as straws in the wind, because they seldom become strong and unequivocal until an upward or downward trend in morale is already well established. The effects of morale are usually diffuse and far reaching, rather than specific or immediate. For example, morale affects the receptivity of employees to being organized by labor unions; their militancy in a union; and the company's employment image, which in turn effects its success in trying to recruit new employees. It also affects the company's ability to retain qualified employees during boom periods when jobs are plentiful elsewhere; and the intangible extras that affect over-all productivity such as cooperation, caution, and craftsmanship.

The overt symptoms of *good* morale are usually quite unspectacular. Relationships tend to be easy and informal. There is banter but little gossip or rumor spreading. Minor deviations in the routines of work are taken in stride and arouse little interest. The humorous comments that are passed around tend to be genial, and no one is singled out as the butt of jokes. When management takes an action that is not immediately understood, the employees usually assume that an adequate explanation will be forthcoming. When morale has *deterio-*

rated, relationships tend to be distant and stiff. Communication takes place within little groups, but not among them, and it is especially limited between management and the rank-and-file employees. There is an atmosphere of suspicion and competition among groups and a tendency to be more concerned with ascribing blame than with solving problems. Rumors tend to persist with or without foundation and linger long after the incident that triggered them has been forgotten. Even trivial events can provoke anger or resentment. Humor tends to be biting and sarcastic, and it is directed either against individuals or specific groups (such as the front office). Unexplained management action is interpreted as hostile, venal, or foolish; and explanations are regarded as alibis.

Good morale is characterized by comfortable relationships that do not get in the way of work, while poor morale is characterized by strained relationships that create an air of impending crisis, and this too often does get in the way of work. At any given time in any given organization, elements of both good and bad morale can probably be found; what matters most is the over-all balance of morale in the organization.

Effects of Morale

Both common sense and experience tell us that the condition of morale has important effects on a company's operating results. But it would be an exaggeration to say that this effect is always *directly* measurable in terms of output or profitability. Unhappy workers are not necessarily unproductive ones, at least in the short run; happy workers are not necessarily good producers. Productivity, profitability, and other measures of operating results are the results of many contributing factors, some of which have their effect more or less immediately and some of which work slowly and indirectly.

It is quite difficult to demonstrate changes in results that are clearly attributable to morale. The skeptic who insists on hard, clearcut proofs will find nothing in the research literature on morale that will dissolve his skepticism. But the manager who realizes that all operating results reflect a great deal more than just their immediate antecedents will find that this same literature provides ample reason for making morale one of his main and continuing concerns. Published studies of the relationship between morale and productivity have yielded varying results, (reflecting the sensitivity of any output statistic to *all* sources of input, whether they happen to be germane to the

research or not). One summary of about two dozen such studies (14) found that in 54 percent of the studies, high morale was reported to be associated with high productivity. In 35 percent of the surveys covered by the review, no relationship was found between the condition of morale and productivity; while high morale was actually associated with *low* productivity in 11 percent of the cases reported.

There are circumstances in which the effect of morale on productivity is fairly direct and others in which it is diluted. In general, where productivity is affected by teamwork, by ingenuity, or by tolerance of adverse conditions, morale will tend to be related to an important degree to what is accomplished. On the other hand, where work is paced by machines or is largely automated, or where labor represents a relatively small part of product cost, or where high productivity in certain crucial departments can largely offset low productivity in others, morale will not tend to have a measurable relationship to operating results. However, an organization must do more than just attain immediate operating results: it must also survive. It must preserve, and if possible enlarge, its resources for obtaining more operating results in the future, which, of course, includes its employees. The same principle that is recognized financially by depletion and depreciation allowances also applies to human resources: the company must not obtain its short-term results at the expense of future results. In this larger sense, morale *always* plays a significant role in company operations.

Morale Trends

Morale is not static. It is subject to daily, or even to momentary, fluctuations, most of which are insignificant. It is also subject to long-term secular trends. These may move upward, downward, or sideways; it is to these that the sophisticated manager pays attention. Significant changes in morale occur slowly, usually over a period of months or even years. These changes reflect the group's gradual adjustment to factors that significantly affect its working environment. These might include such factors as changes in workloads or in work methods, a change in managers or in management philosophy, or even changes in the composition of the work group itself through attrition and new recruiting.

It is useful to think of long-term morale trends as responses to *pressures* and *supports*. A morale pressure is any factor tending over a period of time to reduce morale; for example, a blockage of com-

munications and grievance channels due to inadequate delegation of authority. A morale support is any factor tending over a period of time to raise, or to preserve, morale; for example, a policy of periodically providing employees with new experiences through promotions, transfers, job rotation, or reassignments. Pressures and support are usually present simultaneously in all organizations. It is the preponderance of one over the other that determines the long-term trend of morale. Consequently, the wise manager will be concerned with identifying the significant pressures and supports that are operating in his organization, and with periodically evaluating their relative strength.

As a rule, the information that normally reaches top management about morale tends to be of two kinds. One kind comes from managers who have encountered no glaring or dramatic indications of poor morale and therefore report, honestly but perhaps inaccurately, that all is well. The difficulty arises from the fact that overt indications of poor morale do not tend to become apparent, at least, not unmistakably apparent, until a serious deterioration has already occurred.

The other kind of information that tends to reach top management concerns incidents or individual cases that may suggest that morale is very bad indeed. Sometimes management may react to such indications with an excess of sensitivity, by setting out to reassure people who are not anxious and to assuage people who are not aggrieved. It is perhaps better to do this than to run the risk of a large scale collapse of morale, but it would be even more preferable to know whether incidents are isolated or typical. The larger and more widely dispersed an organization becomes, the more difficult it becomes for management to make this judgment. Its normal sources of information necessarily filter out large masses of facts that do not seem to require top level attention; yet these facts are often the very ones that would present an over-all perspective against which to evaluate reports based on incidents.

The management of any large concern is always sampling the condition of morale through its normal sources. The problem is that this sampling process is more often haphazard than systematic, and the information it provides is seldom representative of morale in the organization as a whole. Sophisticated managements have long recognized this problem and have therefore turned to other, more reliable, means of sampling and measuring morale.

Measuring Morale

Strictly speaking, morale is something we infer about other people's states of mind, and therefore it cannot be measured directly at all. But we can measure some of the effects in which it may be presumed to have played a role. These vary in objectivity from turnover statistics (which are incontestable facts but whose meaning is always somewhat debatable), to depth interviews of the individuals whose morale is under examination (which may get to the heart of the matter, but can also be thoroughly fogged by self-deception or the interviewer's unconscious biases).

There are certain aspects of the working environment that are so obviously related to morale that any sensible manager keeps them under constant surveillance. Among these are compensation (wages or salaries *plus* so-called "fringe" benefits), workloads, the amount of overtime being worked, the average length of exposure to relatively undesirable conditions such as having to remain on call during one's free time, and excessive time away from home on trips. While the importance of each is obvious, there are some less obvious aspects of compensation that deserve further comment.

When people try to evaluate the fairness of their compensation, they usually make several comparisons. First, how much could they expect to be paid for a similar kind of work at another company? Because this comparison is so common, most progressive firms now conduct regular surveys of the wage rates of other comparable companies in the area. When these rates change they may decide to take action to remain competitive with the current wage scale in the local labor market.

Second, individuals consider their compensation relative to that of other people in the same company. This comparison is usually made in terms of the relative importance of various jobs and the kinds of preparation necessary for performing them. When salaries are administered in a haphazard way, charges of favoritism and unfairness are inevitable. Consequently, all sound salary administration programs are based on a formal job evaluation program, in which every job in the company is rated according to certain criteria and then assigned to a suitable category within an over-all structure of rated jobs.

Third, employees consider compensation in terms of their needs.

This calculation is affected by the general relationship of wages to prices, although both bargaining and the normal dynamics of the labor market tend to keep the two in balance. It is also affected by the age of the employees (younger ones and especially those who are newly married tend to have greater needs, relative to their incomes, than older ones) and by their habits with regard to incurring debts.

None of these factors can be taken for granted, especially in view of their sensitivity to external economic conditions and the consequent possibility that what was once a satisfactory situation may become quite unsatisfactory in a matter of months. By keeping in continuous touch with variables such as these, the manager is in a position to prevent a morale support from weakening or a morale pressure from intensifying.

A more formal way of using objective data for the measurement of morale was introduced several years ago by Willard V. Merrihue of General Electric and Raymond A. Katzell of New York University (15). They developed an Employee Relations Index by combining eight objective statistics that tend, as a group, to be correlated with employee attitudes and with productivity. Although a different set of factors may be needed in establishing an effective ERI for different groups of employees, the technique provides a relatively simple early warning system of impending morale difficulties.

Merrihue and Katzell reported one such index that had been worked out for hourly paid employees at several General Electric plants. The factors included in this index were: periods of absence, separations of all types, initial visits to the dispensary for occupational reasons, suggestions submitted through the suggestion system, disciplinary suspensions, formally submitted grievances, work stoppages, and participation in the insurance plan. By using this index, any given plant could be given in ERI "score." These scores in turn were found to be related to the profitability of the plants and also to the kinds of cooperative behavior that makes profitability possible.

A more subjective, yet more sensitive, way of measuring morale consists of scheduled opinion surveys. These are held annually or biannually. In the case of plant populations or other employee groups who work in close proximity to each other, all employees are given an opportunity to participate in each survey. In the case of widely dispersed organizations such as marketing or service groups, a sampling approach may be used. It is always wise to build two safeguards for the employee into every opinion survey, and to adhere to these religiously. One is that participation in the survey be truly *voluntary;*

that is, any employee should be free not to participate, or to participate only partially, if he so desires. The second is that the survey be absolutely *confidential*, that is, the statements contributed by any individual should not be used in a manner that might tend to identify him or even his department. As a rule, flat guarantees on both these points are given at the outset of any survey; yet there are always some people who prefer not to participate. Sometimes this is due to indifference, and sometimes it is due to a fear that an attempt may be made to identify the respondents.

Broadly speaking, there are two opinion survey methods: the interview and the questionnaire. The essential advantage of the interview is its sensitivity and comprehensiveness; that is, it can pick up indications of conditions the interviewer may not have anticipated, and it enables the interviewer to follow up leads thoroughly. The disadvantages of the interview method are that it is uneconomical for use with large groups, and it is to some extent dependent on the interviewer's ability to classify and interpret his data.

The main advantages of the questionnaire method are its economy (it can be given to very large numbers of people in a relatively short time, and the results can be processed by machines, all at modest cost), and its objectivity (the results can be expressed in quantified form and are usually directed comparable to those obtained from other groups or even the same group in a previous survey). The disadvantages of the questionnaire are its insensitivity and lack of comprehensiveness (even the most exhaustive questionnaire may fail to discern trends that authors did not suspect). Because the two methods are essentially complementary, they are often used together. First a sample of people is interviewed to aid in the construction of the questionnaire, then the questionnaire is administered. Follow-up interviews may then be held to explore those topics which may still be unclear.

The analysis of opinion survey data calls first of all for the identification of major pressures and supports. An opinion survey is, after all, useful only to the extent that it is possible to do something about the results. The major responsibility of an opinion survey team is to show management what seems to be causing the present situation. The next responsibility of opinion surveyors is to determine the direction in which morale trends are moving. This requires comparable earlier data from the same group. If previous data are not available, the results may be compared with recent data from another group that is believed to have similar characteristics. The purpose of such

comparisons is to indicate to management whether its previous action has been effective, and at what pace any new action (if any is contemplated) should be introduced.

The third major responsibility of those who conduct an opinion survey is to avoid overgeneralizing and to ensure that management understands the limits of the survey data. If an attitude tends to be characteristic of only a particular subgroup (such as newly hired engineers, or older male clerical workers), it should not be presented in a way that implies that it is characteristic of all employees. Sometimes it is also necessary to point out interaction effects, that is, results that tend to occur only when two or more conditions are present simultaneously. The interpretation of survey data must, in other words, be geared to facilitate effective management action. Survey reports that are merely critical, or merely descriptive without implying a prescription, are of relatively little value to a company. The ultimate purpose of any employee opinion survey is to improve morale, not merely to measure it.

As a rule, employees welcome these surveys and enjoy participating in them. But the welcome wears pretty thin if a number of surveys have been held without any discernable sign that management is being swayed by the results. This is why it is usually wise to give the employees some idea of what the results were. A summary of the survey findings usually suffices to prevent the spread of unrealistic rumors and to satisfy employee curiosity.

Action Plans

Although a downward trend in morale can sometimes be traced to a cause that can be corrected promptly, most often the roots of the problem are harder to excise. In fact, many cases of poor morale are the indirect results of policies that were initiated for reasons having nothing whatever to do with morale. In such cases, a way must be found to revise the policy without subverting its basic aim.

This kind of situation occurred in the clerical departments of a large sales organization. These departments, in which about two thirds of all employees were men, were engaged in processing orders and receiving payments. Although pay was relatively good, career progress was slow since there were only a limited number of managerial openings. An opinion survey was conducted among these employees at a time when there were no overt signs of morale disturbance. The purpose of the survey was purely precautionary, since

management had been impressed with the fact that severe lapses of morale in other departments could probably have been avoided if an adequate early warning system had existed to reveal the underlying deterioration.

The survey in the clerical departments revealed several pertinent facts. Morale among female employees was reasonably high and tended to remain at the same level throughout their careers. There was an annual turnover of about 20 percent, due mostly to marriage and pregnancy, and very few women remained in the company longer than four years. The women appreciated the friendly social relationships on the job, the attractive aspects of the office decor, and the courteous treatment they received from their supervisors. Although their work was detailed and repetitive, they did not complain about it very much. The morale of the newly hired men tended to be very high, but after about a year it began to slip progressively lower. Among the long-service male employees, morale was very low indeed. This trend reflected an initial optimism about career prospects that first turned to skepticism and then to outright pessimism as they recognized the very limited opportunities for promotion that were actually available to them. Turnover among male employees was quite low, due to the relatively high salary scales. Further, new hiring tended to be chiefly of males rather than females, so in effect the proportion of men in these units was rising.

When management examined these results, they drew two important conclusions. The first was that the nature of their business made it unlikely that they could relieve the frustration of the long-service male employees by creating a significant number of new promotional opportunities. The second was that a continuation of the trends revealed by the survey would inevitably increase the proportion of bitter, frustrated men in these departments. Even though no widespread morale problem existed at the time of the survey, it was possible to foresee how one could develop. The policy of hiring more men than women for these jobs was based on a recognition of the higher turnover rate among women and the consequently higher retraining costs. Yet it appeared that in the long run this policy might expose the company to the high costs that a dispirited and frustrated work force can entail.

An effective action plan to resolve this dilemma required, first of all, a sharply-focused view of what the essential problem was. Management decided that, in their zeal to control short-term recruiting and retraining costs, they had been hiring men at a faster rate than

they could be absorbed upward by the organization's relatively slow advancement process. This created an ever-widening backlog of men who, as they became more discouraged, also became less likely candidates for promotion. No action plan is a panacea, but the plan evolved by this company proved to be quite effective. It was a plan for a three-step program. The first was to accelerate the promotion rate, even if only slightly, by creating a greater number of supervisory positions. The second step was to change the hiring mix so as to gradually increase the proportion of women in these departments to about 50 percent. The third step instituted a program of in-service training seminars for all clerical employees.

It is difficult to say which action, or what combination of these actions, was responsible for what happened next; or indeed whether the same outcome might have occurred without any action plan. For practical management purposes, what matters most is that a potential morale crisis never materialized. The morale of the male clerical workers improved; partly in response to the small increase in promotion opportunities and also, more subtly, in response to the lessened competition for promotions that women did not aspire to.

The morale crisis that never occurs is a far more elegant piece of human relations management than resolution of an actual crisis. The prevented crisis leaves no scars, no suspicions, and no animosities. It is a goal well worth seeking. Yet it is also possible to be overzealous in searching out potential morale difficulties and to introduce needless and sometimes costly corrections to nonexistent problems. An example of this type of over reaction occurred in a large engineering organization that employed two main kinds of workers: technicians who repaired and maintained the company's equipment in the field, and sales engineers who custom-designed the equipment to meet the requirements of individual customers. The company had managed, with some difficulty, to weather a period of intense discontent among the technicians. This had been largely due to heavy workloads and excessive overtime work.

The company had recognized this problem rather belatedly, and in order to rectify it had engaged in a heavy hiring and training program that increased its staff of technicians. As the rumblings of dissatisfaction subsided among the technicians, management began to eye its sales engineers rather nervously. Although there were no overt signs of a morale problem, these men were known to be struggling with heavy workloads and long hours. Might they not be on the verge of the same kind of open conflict that the technicians had just experienced? If so, it would not be so easy to set matters straight. Qualified

engineers were in short supply. Further, their salaries were considerably higher than those of the technicians; since the company had already strained its resources in correcting the technicians' problem, it could ill afford to hire many new sales engineers.

It appeared that if the sales engineers felt unhappy about their workload, they would simply have to endure it. Therefore management searched for a way to alleviate the engineers' predicament. A plan was devised to pay all sales engineers a sizable surprise bonus. Although the men were already well paid and the company could ill-afford the added expenditure, this was deemed preferable to having to undergo the same sort of disturbance that had racked the technicians. However, before a final decision was reached on the bonus plan, it was decided to conduct an opinion survey among the sales engineers. This revealed three significant findings: The general level of morale in this group was good, and there was no sign of an impending deterioration; most men were reasonably satisfied with their current pay levels; and most intriguing of all, there was a positive correlation between workload and morale; that is, the men who were putting in the longest hours tended to feel the greatest degree of satisfaction with the company and their jobs.

Further investigation showed that most of the sales engineers found their jobs intriguing, challenging, and absorbing. In a word, they loved their work. While it demanded a great deal of their time, they were quite willing to give it; in fact, at least some of their overtime hours were due to inability to leave a particularly fascinating technical problem. Because their work was essentially creative rather than routine, the sales engineers derived a great deal of satisfaction from their work. Management quietly shelved its plan for a surprise bonus. It was clearly unnecessary. While the sales engineers would undoubtedly have been delighted to receive it, they neither wanted nor needed a bonus. The problem it was intended to correct did not exist. The jobs of the technicians and the sales engineers were sufficiently different that what was true of one group did not necessarily apply to the other. In fact, management's principal action as a result of the opinion survey of its sales engineers was to begin a study of how to increase the opportunities for individual creativity in the work of its technicians.

Management of Human Relations

By now it should be apparent that developing an effective management response to a serious human relations problem is a difficult,

costly, and usually imperfect process. For this reason, sophisticated managements are placing less emphasis on their ability to *respond* to problems and more on their ability to anticipate and *prevent* problems. This philosophy is at the core of modern human relations management.

In large measure, this calls for implementing sound human relations policies by assuring that effective communications loops are maintained, by providing adequate grievance channels, and by seeing to it that first-line management works fairly and understandingly with employees. It calls for equitable compensation policies, realistic career planning, and a good appraisal and counseling program. It also requires that the condition and causes of morale be periodically measured and analyzed.

The measurement and analysis of morale makes possible an intelligent adaptation to changing currents of satisfaction and dissatisfaction. It enables management to detect and resolve little problems befor they turn into big ones. It permits an evaluation of the effects of previous management action. Most important of all, it keeps management in touch with current trends in employee thinking and thereby avoids the kind of "management by nostalgia" that so often occurs when an organization changes more rapidly than its leaders realize.

The effective management of human relations—to return to the thought with which we opened Chapter One—is not merely *possible* in the light of what behavioral research has revealed, it is also *essential* in the light of our rapidly evolving social and political order. Although it will probably not become a science in our lifetime, it has long since become an art to which every manager can profitably, and enjoyably, devote himself.

SELECTED READINGS

Chapter 1. For a review of the development of the concept of industrial democracy, see Berle, A. A., Jr. *The Twentieth Century Capitalist Revolution.* New York: Harcourt, 1954.

For an analysis of the effects of wage incentives, especially on factory workers, see Whyte, W. F. *Money and Motivation.* New York: Harper & Row, 1955.

Chapter 2. For a general review of economic history, see Heilbroner, R. *The Making of Economic Society.* Englewood Cliffs, N.J.: Prentice-Hall, 1962.

Chapter 3. For a retrospective analysis of the Hawthorne study and the many experiments and critiques it inspired, see Landsberger, H. *Hawthorne Revisited.* Ithaca, N.Y.: Cornell University Press, 1958.

For a general summary of research by the Institute for Social Research and the theory that has evolved from its work, see Likert, R. *New Patterns of Management.* New York: McGraw-Hill, 1961.

Chapter 4. For the best introduction to Argyris' theories, see Argyris, C. *Personality and Organization.* New York: Harper & Row, 1957.

For the best introduction to McGregor's theories, see McGregor, D. *The Human Side of Enterprise.* New York: McGraw-Hill, 1960.

Chapter 5. For a practical and succinct review of what research has shown about the internal communication systems of organizations, see Peterfreund, S. *Upward Communication in Problem Solving.* New York: Douglas Williams Associates, 1964.

Chapter 6. For a review of grievance procedures under union contracts, see Herron, John S., Jr. Negotiating and Administering the Grievance Procedure, in Marting, E. (ed.) *Understanding Collective Bargaining,* New York: American Management Association, 1958.

Chapter 7. For an analysis of the problems involved in implementing a performance appraisal program, see Kellogg, Marion S. New Angles in Appraisal. In T. Whisler and S. Harper (eds.) *Performance Appraisal: Research and Practice.* New York: Holt, Rinehart and Winston, 1962.

In the same volume, see also Maier, N. R. F. Three Types of Appraisal Interview.

Chapter 8. For a general review of the acquisition of competence and achievement motives, see White, R. W. Motivation Reconsidered: The Concept of Competence. *Psychological Review* 66:5, 1959; and McClelland, D. C. *The Achieving Society.* Princeton, N.J., Van Nostrand, 1961.

For a review of the practical problems involved in financing retirement plans, see Faltermayer, E. K. The Drift to Early Retirement. *Fortune,* May, 1965.

Chapter 9. For a review of the practical aspects of the absenteeism problem, see Gaudet, F. *Solving the Problems of Employee Absence.* New York: American Management Association, Research Study No. 57, 1963.

For an analysis of wartime industrial absenteeism, see Mayo, E. *The Social Problems of an Industrial Civilization,* Boston: Harvard Business School, 1945.

Chapter 10. For a general discussion of morale, see Gellerman, S. *Motivation and Productivity,* New York: American Management Association, 1963.

BIBLIOGRAPHY

1. Blum, Albert A. *Management and the White Collar Union.* New York: American Management Association, 1964.
2. *The Trade Union Situation in the United States.* Report of a Mission from the International Labor Office. Geneva, 1960.
3. Likert, Rensis. *New Patterns of Management.* New York: McGraw-Hill, 1961.
4. Gellerman, S. W. *Motivation and Productivity.* New York: American Management Association, 1963.
5. Greenewalt, Crawford H. *The Uncommon Man.* New York: McGraw-Hill, 1959.
6. Cordiner, Ralph J. *New Frontiers for Professional Managers.* New York: McGraw-Hill, 1956.
7. Watson, Thomas J., Jr. *A Business and Its Beliefs.* New York: McGraw-Hill, 1964.
8. Peterfreund, Stanley. Communications in action. *Bell Telephone Magazine,* Summer 1963.
9. Smith, Richard Austin. *Corporations In Crisis.* New York: Doubleday, 1964.
10. Revans, R. W. *Standards for Morale, Cause and Effect in Hospitals.* London: Oxford University Press, 1964.

11. Sirota, David. *The Effect of Adequate Grievance Channels on Reactions to MIP (Methods Improvement Program).* Unpublished study, General Products Division, IBM Corporation, 1962.
12. McGregor, Douglas. An uneasy look at performance appraisal. *Harvard Business Review,* May-June 1957.
13. Mayfield, Harold. In defense of performance appraisal. *Harvard Business Review,* March-April 1960.
14. Herzberg, F., B. Mausner, R. Peterson, D. Capwell. *Job Attitudes: Review of Research and Opinion.* Pittsburgh: Psychological Service of Pittsburgh, 1957.
15. Merrihue, W. V., and R. S. Katzell, ERI, Yardstick of employee relations. *Harvard Business Review,* 33:6, November-December 1955.

Index